What Others Are Saying about HEARING VOICES . . .

Paul Surace is an extraordinarily empathetic and insightful writer who brings humor and truth to the craft. His characters are always compelling in their painful, compassionate, messy realness. His plays will teach you something about your relationships, yourself, and about what it means to be human.

— *Stephanie Storey, Author of the Novel "Oil and Marble."*

The strength of Paul Surace's writing is in the characters he creates. They're richly felt and deeply human, and they reveal the importance of seeing ourselves for our strengths rather than our weaknesses.

— *Matt Healy, Psychotherapist, Screenwriter for "Clay Pigeons"*

Paul Surace's writing is consistently entertaining, thought provoking, and insightful. With each play, he taps into the human experience by penetrating the deep layers of the issues we deal with. He does it with humor, pathos, and integrity. His audiences walk away with insight, laughter, and a rousing awareness of their own vulnerabilities. This collection will inspire you, make you laugh and make you think. A great formula for enjoyable theater.

—*Fran Montano, Artistic Director, The Actor's Workout Studio*

For more than a decade, I've had the privilege of observing and learning from Paul's work as a dedicated psychotherapist. He has given us all a gift choosing to share, in dramatic form, the insights into humanity gained from his clinical experience. This collection of plays is really a set of decisive and defining moments for characters we've all engaged with. These complex individuals are drawn by their author with kindness and authenticity.

— *Michael Llach, Psychotherapist*

Paul's plays deliver a wonderful mix of humor and heart.

— *Dagney Kerr, Writer, Actress*

Paul R. Surace / HEARING VOICES

Thankfully, Paul Surace has published an anthology of his theatrical works. Surace has managed the task of penning both comedy and tragedy, a daunting task to say the least. Enjoy the ride through each one of his works; the results will be sublime*!*

— *George Kappaz, Psychotherapist*

Surace's writing hits home on so many levels. It's instantly personal, poignant and thought provoking. He tackles themes that examine love and relationships, the family dynamic, and the ever-evolving journey to solve the human condition . . . and manages to handle all of it with integrity, honesty and truth. His writing is accessible, and his dialogue is so natural that you feel like you've had the same conversations in your own life multiple times over. He creates characters that every actor would want to embody and stories that every reader would want to experience.

— *Frank Licari, Actor, Writer, Producer*

Paul's work, like the author himself, is easy to love. Kind, gentle, honest and endearing, his words bring a beating heart to every moment of conflict and clarity in his characters' lives. . .and in doing so, he helps each of us, as actors and audience, find the humor in our pain and the love in our loss.

--- *Jylian Sy, Actor, Writer, Producer*

Paul's plays are a heartfelt, entertaining, and fun journeys into relationships. Candid, unpretentious, and relatable. There is something here for everyone.   — *Chris Karmiol, Actor, Writer*

Paul Surace's characters are extremely likeable, very human, and a real joy for actors and directors alike to develop, interpret, and see come to life onstage.

— *Dolores Aguanno, Actor, Director, Producer*

A Paul Surace play is loaded with humor, humanity, and realism. Guaranteed to strike a chord with audience members. I've had the pleasure/honor of acting in two of his productions. And afterwards, I discovered that I learned a little bit more about myself.

— *Roger Gutierrez, Actor, Writer*

What Others Are Saying. . .

Paul's writing is fun and endearing, his stories and words ooze innocence and purity, even the heavier stories. That's not easy to do! It reminds me of how Spielberg directs, capturing the essence of goodness in darkness.

— *Chris Roland, Change Agent, Author, Speaker, Filmmaker ("Darfur," "Stander," and "The Forgotten Kingdom")*

Surace writes with gusto, heft, and precision. These are characters we all know...they populate our family, our work, our friendships. They're familiar, and in Surace's hand, they resonate with authenticity and with humanity.

— *Daniel T. Green, Ph.D., Director, Master of Entertainment Industry Management Program, Carnegie Mellon University.*

Paul Surace understands the complexities of human behavior. He creates layered characters that impact each other to create powerful scenes. Paul has a way of shining light on the darkest part of family relationships, while always giving us a glimmer of hope. Every reader will see something of their family (and themselves) in these plays. But please don't think it's devoid of humor. Paul is a very funny writer, mining comedy from human relationships and expectations. One may think Paul suffers from mood swings, but he's just in touch with the spectrum of human emotions. And you will be, too, once you've read his plays.

— *Tom Misuraca, novelist ("Lifestyles of the Damned") and Award-Winning Playwright.*

Paul Surace's work as a playwright and therapist is nothing short of exquisite. He brings such insight, compassion and wit into his stories making them beautifully relatable. The lessons learned through the characters in Paul's stories provide such valuable wisdom for all.

— *Traci Maffei, Psychotherapist*

ISBN-13: 978-0692161937
ISBN-10: 0692161937

Library of Congress Control Number: 2018959526

Printed in United States of America
        For more information contact:
        paulnywriter@gmail.com
        www.CandlelightPlays.com

Publishing Company: Candlelight Plays
Cover Illustration: Jeffrey Vernon
Editing: Cary Editorial
Author Photo: Rickie Peete

DEDICATION

To my parents, Andrew and Marie Surace
And to my lovely wife, Nathalie

HEARING VOICES

15 Short Plays
by a Psychotherapist

Paul Richard Surace, LMFT

Don't curse the darkness, light a candle.
— *Confucius*

Candlelight Plays
Los Angeles, California

CONTENTS

ACKNOWLEDGEMENTS

My Wife NATHALIE whose love for me, for her family, and for many others has inspired me to be a more open and loving person. She's been patient and generous in allowing me the time to be creative with my writing, producing, and performing of my work while I continue working full-time asa psychotherapist. She's also been a creative muse during our shared life together and has been the inspiration for several of the plays found in this book.

My "go to" director, CONRAD DUNN, who has directed many of the scenes you will read in this book. Mentor, and personal friend, Conrad is one of the most "reasonable" men I've met in show business. He's thoughtful, articulate, and kind in his direction and treatment of actors and this writer's work. He's a man who early in his career, ran a theatre company for ten years, and went on to make a living at TV and film acting for 35 years afterwards.

Artistic Director, FRAN MONTANO, founder of the Actor's Workout Studio in North Hollywood, California. Fran's a man who believes in nurturing creativity and creating synergy between his writers and the actors that study at his theatre. Perhaps that is why he has undertaken to sponsor so many productions that have been created from the material generated by the Writer's group that is housed at his theatre. Fran's generosity was in large part responsible for inspiring writers like myself to keep on working their craft and creating scripts and scenes that could potentially be produced at his theatre (and into books like this one).

The many TALENTED DIRECTORS who guided the actors, did the blocking and stagecraft, and carried a vision for my scenes that brought my words to life in a believable and powerful way: Conrad Dunn, Dolores Aguanno, Kelly Stables Patino, Stacy Ann Raposa, Katy Pollock Iva, Paul Winfield Ehrlich, Louise Kroot-Haukka, Freddy Gonzales, Rickie Peete, Paul Storiale, Tim Simek, Ali Kendall, Kaz Matamura, and Laurie Nelson-Scarpelli.

The many EXCITING ACTORS that gave flesh and blood and voice to my imagined characters: Dagney Kerr, Sarah Ambrosio, Maria Moreno, Greg Yoder, Paula LaFayette,Justin Bryant Rapp, Ana Valverde, Holger Moncada, Jr.,Brent Harvey, Mitchell DeGuzman, Jessie Navarro-Parks, Ben Solenberger, William Sterling, Robert DiTillio, Cliff Weissman, Jylian Sy, Chris Guerrero, Emma Travis, Devin Caldarone, Allegra Williams, Nick Dostal, Kiki Aldonas, Danny Christensen, Paula Lafayette, Darren Mangler, Katy Pollock Iva, Ronnie Rose, Julie Dolan, Chris Karmiol, Susan Smythe Robinson, Catherine Mersereau, Eric Chaefsky, Mariel Suriel, Warren G. Hall, Sebastiano Pestoni, Kent Hatch, Roger Gutierrez, Tony DeCarlo, John- Paul Lavoisier, Patricia Canale, and Gregory Niebel.

Book Editor, SYLVIA CARY, also a psychotherapist and a friend, who encouraged me to take a large portion of my theatrical work—and finally publish it into this first book of plays. And guided me every step of the way—solving problems and editing the prose sections found in the book.

Acknowledgements

My Parents, ANDREW and MARIE, with no more than high-school educations raised four smart, productive and independent children. They taught us to dream big and reach for the stars, but also to keep our feet planted firmly on the ground while doing so. Early on, they made it clear to us that life didn't owe us anything, and we'd better work hard to achieve our goals. They pushed us to get "real" careers that would make us financially stable as we pursued our creative gifts in our spare time. Most of all, my parents modeled for us the idea of never giving up, even when times get rough.

Playwriting influences: (to name a few) Arthur Miller, Paddy Chaefsky, Rod Serling, Tennesee Williams, Neil Simon, August Wilson, Athol Fugard, David Mamet, and John Patrick Shanley.

Finally, I would like to thank my many psychotherapist colleagues, golfing buddies, high-school and grad school friends who have faithfully attended my theatrical shows over the years. And for all those friends who couldn't attend, and instead wrote kind and encouraging words of support onto my Facebook page, you know who you are, and I thank you also. All these good folks inspire me to keep writing and producing my work.

FOREWORD

It is with a great deal of trepidation that I've taken on the task of providing the foreword for this collection of Paul Surace's plays.

I am inordinately invested in this being a successful endeavor, which would mean if you happened to be sitting on the fence about getting his book, by the time you finish reading this foreword you'll decide you've GOT TO HAVE IT! The reason I want you to get it (beyond the fact that all the plays in this collection are GOOD) is that I like it when good things happen to good people, and Mr. Surace is one of the finest human beings it's been my privilege to have met in this life. He's a throwback kind of a guy, in his life, and in his writing. He's a gentleman, fully embodying the origin of that word, *gentle man*. It is reflected in every one of his plays; there are always characters you care about, always someone to pull for, no anti-heroes here.

When I first had the good fortune to work on one of his plays, I remarked at the time that his writing had in it an "old school" sensibility to it, very much along the lines of Frank Capra who always wrote about the little guy, the struggles inherent in living an unprivileged life, the rewards that can be had by being true to your beliefs, and never giving up no matter what the outcome — knowing you did your best and maintained your humanity. Those of a cynical bent called it Capra corn, but his work lives on, and is beloved. There is a similar quality to Paul's writing. In it, you will find human beings, with all their foibles, but always striving to do their best, and be their best, whatever their circumstances, whatever their shortcomings. And we care about them and pull for them because they're just like us, and we want for them what we want for ourselves, to be happy and appreciated.

Now march yourself over to the check-out and get this book. You'll be doing something for someone else, as well as for yourself. It's a win-win, and isn't that the way we'd like life to be? So make it *so*, starting right here, right now.

— *Conrad Dunn*

INTRODUCTION

I fell in love with the theatre early in life. Two plays stand out in my mind as being primarily responsible for enticing me into and onto the world of the stage. The first was reading Arthur Miller's *"Death of a Salesman"* while in high-school; the second was experiencing an audience's reaction to watching one of my own plays.

When I first read *"Death of a Salesman,"* I was so profoundly impacted by Willy Loman's tragic demise that I lay in my bed and cried for quite some time after finishing it. I remember wishing that I could have intervened or talked with the character of Willy Loman, and helped him to see things differently so that he would not take the route he did. But as a reader I was helpless to do anything but take the sad ride along with him. Miller's play inspired me to try to write the same kind of emotionally powerful stories that he had written, but perhaps more hopeful. That led me to take it upon myself to write, produce, and perform in the annual Christmas play for my Evangelical church in Long Island, New York. When I heard the laughter and excited whispers from that church audience during the performance of my play, I felt the *power* of my own words come to life and was forever changed by it. I was hooked. Through theatre, I had finally found a way of expressing my thoughts and feelings to others.

I must have attended close to fifty Broadway productions prior to leaving New York for a Hollywood writing career with Walt Disney Company in the late nineties. I'd also read, performed, or participated in productions of more than a hundred other plays.

What I find so exciting about theatre is the idea of seeing people "caught in the act" of struggling to do the right thing—by each other and their principles. I want to see it all played out before me, and not just be told about how it had happened in the past—or present—which is more of a classroom experience. What happens in a production (whether it's mounted on Broadway or at a local community theatre) is that the words, stories, and characters are brought to life. You frequently see people caught up in desperate situations which are acted out right in front of you. The characters that you end up caring about must figure a way out of their risky plight by the time the play is over. But perhaps the greatest blessing of theatre is that *theatrical* stories are condensed so that they will almost always build to a climactic finish in a relatively short period of time. It is precisely this dramatic shrinking of a story's timeline that infuses it with the ability to impact the audience and stir their deepest feelings—which happens only infrequently in real life.

Looking back on it, my Broadway *education* got me a front row seat to see some of theatre's most memorable characters on stage working out life's challenges from a vantage point that went way beyond my New York Italian upbringing or the Evangelical church I grew up in. It was the theatre that allowed me to see past the smaller, more isolated, and parochial world that I'd been raised in. I was provided with valuable insights that helped me make more sense out of life, and eventually led me to find a greater peace within my conflicted self. It's not hard to see why this kind of exposure to different kinds of people and beliefs helped me to be less judgmental and more accepting of differences in others, and more accepting of myself. Theatre helped me to listen with a more open heart to the people who would make themselves vulnerable by sharing with me their stories they deemed important to tell. And in that sense, it was also a great preparation for me to enter into the field of psychotherapy.

The 15 plays in this book are in fact *my* stories that I've deemed worthy of telling you. As a writer, I've tried to the best of my ability to *hear the voices* of my characters, many of whom feel lost, stuck in a dismal world, and hopeless to change. It is my hope that you will laugh, and cry, and be inspired by these stories. Rest assured, there will be more to come. Enjoy!

— Paul Richard Surace

CHAPTER 1 — FAMILY

CHAPTER 1 — FAMILY

Most anything has the power to change you — but in this first volume of plays, I've focused on the following four agents of change: *Family, Friendship, Love, and Redemption.*

In psychotherapy, the family usually gets credit for informing or creating the major part of one's personality. This happens primarily through the constructs of NATURE and NURTURE.

Nature is the genetic component that comes to each of us courtesy of our parents and accounts for our basic wiring—gender, personality, natural gifts or strengths, blind spots or challenged areas, body type, eye color, and certain genetic-linked mental health issues. Research shows us that such conditions as depression, anxiety, bi-polar, schizophrenia, autism, and others may have a genetic link passed down through the genes which can influence the way we interpret and/or "filter" the world around us. On a happier note, the same thing seems to be true for many creative gifts and talents. Children seem to inherit many of the passions of the parents. Think of how many actors, writers, singers, dancers, and musicians have children who grow up and use the gifts they've been given to enter into the same field as their parents. It can't just be a coincidence.

Nurture refers to the environment one is born into and grows up in. This, too, plays a great part in forming a person. The most influential environment is usually the FAMILY we're raised in and how those particular parents choose to raise their children. Other major influencers will include sibling relationships and the factors that influence the quality of those relationships (i.e. how many siblings, years apart, are they supportive, competitive, or bullying towards one another). Also, one is influenced by the religious and cultural background offered up by parents as part of the package. The surrounding neighborhood, the schools attended, and the types of friends made will also have an impact and help determine a child's character. Hopefully the child will also be offered opportunities to nurture their gifts and develop healthy self-esteem, rather than being subjected to negative influences, criticism, and/or abuse—which may have a smothering and limiting impact.

That said, all of us will most likely have to work through both the positive and the negative influences that have come our way whether through our genes and environment — through our nature and nurture. Fortunately, people can be remarkably resilient and find all kinds of ways to heal themselves from any early wounding. Supportive and loving relationships, for example, can help a great deal, as can religion(s) or spiritual practice, sports, yoga, meditation, mentors, supportive friends, and therapy. Exposure to literature, movies, and television which show children solid role-models and promote healthy and happy lifestyles can also play a pivotal role in healing.

Now, let the plays begin!

FATHER'S DAY
A short play — Drama

CAST OF CHARACTERS:
NICK: Late 20's thru 30's, a therapist with unresolved issues with his father. Married to Lauren.
LAUREN: Late 20' thru 30's, rule-oriented, married to Nick.

SETTING: Inside Nick's Man-cave (i.e., living room or office).
TIME: Father's Day. Mid-afternoon.

Originally produced as part of *New York State of Mind—Volume* III at Actor's Workout Studio in North Hollywood, CA. Opened on October 14th, 2016.
Directed by Conrad Dunn.

The cast was as follows:
NICK: Greg Yoder
LAUREN: Paula LaFayette

FATHER'S DAY

The stage is in black for a moment, and then we hear SFX of a "flick" that comes from a cigarette lighter. And suddenly, a flame burns from the lighter for a moment, lighting up a man's face who's sitting on a couch. The man with the lighter is NICK and he holds the flame close to his cigar but doesn't light it up. A moment passes, and then a Woman's voice calls out.

LAUREN: *(OFFSTAGE.)* Nick... Nicky... Where are you?
(The door opens, revealing LAUREN, an attractive woman who turns on the lights for this room. NICK shades his eyes from the sudden glare of the overhead lights. He looks towards LAUREN and snuffs out the flame of his lighter.)

NICK: That's a little bright, Lauren.

LAUREN: Sorry. *(She sees the cigar in his hand.)* You weren't going to light that up in here.

NICK: No, Sir. I know the rules.

LAUREN: You know that's what the balcony's for.

NICK: Lauren, I said that I know the rules.

LAUREN: Okay then. Why are you in here *alone*—with your cigar?

NICK: You make it sound so twisted when you say it like that.

LAUREN: Well, you know what they say about cigars.

NICK: Screw Freud. You know sometimes *a cigar, is just a cigar.*

LAUREN: That's right. And you like smoking cigars. Despite the research that shows it could cause lip, throat, and mouth cancer.

NICK: Yes, thank you very much for sharing the *research* with me.

LAUREN: You know Freud died of throat cancer?

NICK: Yes, I knew that. And screw Freud already.

LAUREN: Okay, Let's forget him, but you may want to call your mother. She called earlier to wish you a happy Father's Day.

NICK: Is that a joke? We don't have any kids.

LAUREN: I think she just wanted to acknowledge you as one of her kids. You had a father, and she was married to him. And she also mentioned that you hadn't called her in a few weeks.

NICK: Oh. She threw that in for good measure, huh?

LAUREN: You really should call her.

NICK: I said I'd call. And by the way, having kids doesn't make you a father.

LAUREN: Huh? What's that?

NICK: Forget it... uh... Didn't you say you were leaving?

LAUREN: You want me to go?

NICK: Or you could stay, and then I'll go out to the balcony for a smoke.

LAUREN: You'd rather smoke than talk with me about this?

NICK: A cigar doesn't argue with me. Lauren. Or talk to me like I'ma kid.

LAUREN: Fine. Go ahead and smoke. And be just like your father.

(NICK reacts to this remark.)

LAUREN: I'm sorry. I didn't mean that.

NICK: Then why'd you say it?

LAUREN: Cause you told me your father smoked a lot of cigars. Alone.

NICK: That's right.

LAUREN: And you told me your father seemed lonely.

NICK: He was.

LAUREN: And I don't want that for you.

NICK: You think I'm lonely?

LAUREN: You have friends. People you like at your work. I just don't see you talking to them. Making plans with them.

NICK: We've been through this already, Lauren.

LAUREN: We have? Then explain it to me again.

NICK: The married ones all have families. Doing things with their kids and staying busy. And the single guys are busy trying to hook up with someone, so they can start a family or get laid. Either way, I don't know if you got the research on this, but nobody's looking for new *friends*, especially at our age.

LAUREN: Oh my God. You make us sound so old.

NICK: We're not ancient but. . . what can I say.

LAUREN: Okay. Let's just say you're mostly right on this. Good friends aren't easy to come by.

NICK: So you do concede my point.

LAUREN: Yes, and then maybe we should talk about starting a family of our own. And stay *busy* like everyone else. Think of all the new couples we can meet at school or with you coaching our kids in sports.

NICK: Oh man, you're good. You just took me down with a judo move where you agree with me rather than fight me, and turn my own aggressive force against me. Masterful work, Sensei, but I'm not interested in having the "we should have kids now" talk.

LAUREN: Okay, fine, but in the end—

BOTH: *All you have is family.*

LAUREN: You say that like it's a bad thing.

NICK: It's not the truth. Not what I experienced.

LAUREN: Your dad had issues.

NICK: My dad got screwed over in business by his two brothers that he brought into his business. These would be the same two uncles I never saw or spoke to again when things went bad between them. So much for the *all you have is family* bullshit.

LAUREN: He never forgave them.

NICK: I don't blame him. How do you screw the guy that sets you up to make a living and feed your family?

LAUREN: So what do *you* blame him for?

NICK: You know that he and his brothers built something like five hundred homes all around LaGuardia airport?

LAUREN: You told me. Before they had their falling out.

NICK: I was thinking maybe he would show me a few of those homes and brag to me a little about what he'd done when he was in his prime.

LAUREN: Your father was quite successful.

NICK: Yes, he was, and I flew home into damn LaGuardia a dozen times while I was away at college.

LAUREN: He never showed you any?

NICK: Never even picked me up from the airport. Mom felt bad and she'd make excuses for him. She tried to pay me for the two busses it took to get my ass home to Long Island, but I didn't take her money.

LAUREN: I'm sorry, Nick, you deserved—

NICK: —STOP, Lauren! It's not about what I deserved.

LAUREN: Then what's your point? What are you saying?

NICK: After I graduated, I didn't come home much after that. I'd resigned myself to what it was between us. And the years went by and he got to be an old man, and then you and I hooked up, and you talked me into going home to see him. . . *It's about family, Nick Make your peace with your dad, Nick, while you still can.*

LAUREN: And you did that. We went to your home and I got to meet him, and you made your peace.

NICK: And he liked you. You were sweet with him and made him laugh and he even got silly around you sometimes. All the things he never was with me. And it was like—me with my degree in psychology—what did it mean to him? *Hey Dad, I'm licensed now; doing good honest work, making a decent wage, helping the world be*

11

a better place. It all meant nothing to him until you came along, and then he lights up like a Christmas candle with you by my side. And he presses a *re*do button on our relationship.

LAUREN: So you made peace with him that day, Nick. I saw that.

NICK: Did you, Lauren? . . . Did you see when he invited me out on the patio to smoke one of those cheap-ass cigars with him? Cause that's something he'd never done before. I mean the guy never taught me a sport or a hobby, never took me fishing or for a game of golf or even bought me lunch for that matter. And then I bring you home with me, and now he wants to share a goddamn cigar with me? *Now*, I'm finally man enough to smoke a cigar with him?!

LAUREN: I think you've got this all wrong, Nick. He was probably looking at me, thinking I'm going to give him some babies, right . . . grand-kids he can spoil rotten.

NICK: Maybe so, but let me finish. So he invites me out to the patio for a smoke. And I told 'em, *"No thanks, Pops, not today."* But I think what I was really saying to the guy was. . .

(He can't complete the sentence. She sits next to him and takes his hand in hers.)

LAUREN: Nicky, you're *not* your father.

NICK: I keep telling myself that. I got help. I talked to people about what I didn't get from him. I went to grad school and wrote a lot of papers trying to make more sense of it. Became this therapist that helps people with their family problems. I did all that . . . maybe to prove to myself that I wasn't him.

LAUREN: Isn't that enough, honey? You did a lot of work to understand your past, but it seems like you're still stuck in it.

NICK: I disagree. I'm not stuck, Lauren, but sometimes I just want to talk to the guy. *(Looks at the cigar in his hand.)* Grab a smoke with him, and let him know that I understand him better now.

LAUREN: I see.

NICK: *(re: cigar)* I think I want to light this sucker up.

LAUREN: Sure.

(She kisses him gently on the lips, and then rises from the couch and begins crossing towards the door. She suddenly turns back to him.)

LAUREN: And if you want to smoke in here, in your man-cave, then have at it. All rules are off today, Nicky. . . It's Father's Day. *(Smiles at him.)*

NICK: Yes, it is. . . Thanks Babe. Could you shut the light on the way out?

*(She nods her understanding and turns off the light as she exits. And the room goes dark for a moment. Again, we hear the same **SFX** as before—it's the FLICK of a lighter.*

13

And again, we see a single flame rising from the lighter which burns bright for a moment as it moves towards NICK's cigar, as we . . .)

FADE LIGHTS.
END PLAY.

FAKEBOOK FRIENDS
A short play — Comedy

CAST OF CHARACTERS:
ANTHONY: NY Italian. Late 20's/early 30's. Married to Gloria.
GLORIA: Latina, Late 20's/early 30's. Married to Anthony.

SETTING: Queens, New York Apartment. Dining/Living Room Table.
TIME: Present moment. Evening.

Originally produced as part of **New York State of Mind—Volume II** at Actor's Workout Studio in North Hollywood, CA. Opened on June 6[th,] 2014.
Directed by Louise Kroot-Haukka.

The cast was as follows:
ANTHONY: Justin Bryant Rapp
GLORIA: Ana Valverde

FAKEBOOK FRIENDS

We're inside a small apartment in Queens, New York. ANTHONY sits at his dining room table in front of his open laptop computer—intensely focused on the task at hand. He's reading out loud from his laptop screen.

ANTHONY: Do I confirm this? HELL YES, I confirm this! HASTA LA VISTA, BABY!

(Forcefully, ANTHONY taps a button on his laptop keyboard, just as GLORIA enters the room, holding a Dora & Diego bedspread in her hands.)

ANTHONY: YES! I confirm this already! Bye, Bye, BEE-ATCH!

(Again, He taps a button on his keyboard, and smiles as he stays focused on computer screen.)

GLORIA: Anthony, why are you cursing at your computer?

(ANTHONY holds up his hand to silence her. And now, she holds up the colorful bedspread to him.)

GLORIA: Did you see what I got my nephew for his birthday? He loves watching Dora & Diego, so I got him a bedspread. And it comes with a matching pillow-case.

ANTHONY: *(Ignoring her.)* Fantastic! Pillowcases are great.

GLORIA: You didn't even look up. Honey, what are you doing?

ANTHONY: No, I got it babe. Dora—Diego—pillow-cases —it's all *muy bien* as you would say it, but I've got to stay focused here.

(GLORIA grows more curious about what he's doing, puts down the bedspread and crosses to him at table— until she's looking over his shoulder at the laptop screen. He taps a few more keys, and begins reading from the screen again.)

ANTHONY: Oh yeah—absolutely confirmed! SO LONG SUCKER! (*With a flourish, he clicks another key on his computer's keypad.*)

GLORIA: Anthony, who are you calling *sucker*? What are you doing?

ANTHONY: Baby, I'm asking you to stay out of this. Please.

(She takes a closer look at his laptop screen.)

GLORIA: Are you de-friending someone from your Facebook?

ANTHONY: Technically, no.

GLORIA: How is it *no* when I see you doing this?

ANTHONY: First off, it's not just one person, it's a lot of people. Second, these were not my friends. They were . . . *(Said with great disgust.) Facebook* friends.

17

GLORIA: Am I hearing you to say that that they are your friends on the Facebook, but they are NOT *your* friends? I am confused. If not your friends, then whose friends were they?

ANTHONY: These people don't even qualify as Facebook friends. They were FAKE-book friends.

GLORIA: What's gotten into you?

ANTHONY: Nothing. It's what I'm taking *out* of me that matters now. Cause this is just like pulling weeds from a garden or chopping out the dead wood from my forest.

GLORIA: So tell me then—*Quien*? Just WHO is it that you're pulling out of your forest?

ANTHONY: Forget about the forest, Gloria. Let's just simplify, and call it a spring cleaning.

GLORIA: Okay then. Just who is it that you're *spring cleaning* from your Facebook?

ANTHONY: Well . . . My lame-ass brother for one.

GLORIA: *QUE?! Tu hermano?*

ANTHONY: Yes, and my niece. Oh, and my cousin too.

GLORIA: Tony, why are you de-friending your family? *Estas loco*?!

ANTHONY: Look, nobody gets a free pass from me just cause they're family. Screw that!

GLORIA: Did you try and talk to them first? And let them know what you were thinking?

ANTHONY: No, I didn't.

GLORIA: Well, I don't understand this.

ANTHONY: Is it really so hard for you to understand that I've reached a point in my life where I want to take stock of who my *true* friends really are?

GLORIA: Okay then. So how many *true* friends have you got left on Facebook?

ANTHONY: What difference does that make?

GLORIA: Like you just said—it's good to know who your true friends really are- so let's start with a number. How many?

ANTHONY: Before or after the spring cleaning?

GLORIA: *AFTER! DESPUES! ESTE MOMENTO!*

ANTHONY: On Facebook?

GLORIA: Yes, on the Facebook! We're talking about Facebook. How many?

ANTHONY: . . . Two.

GLORIA: *Two?* (*Trying to stifle her laughter.*) Two friends? That's it?

ANTHONY: You heard right. And it's not funny.

GLORIA: You're right. This is serious. (*She smiles wide.*) Two friends. Who are they?

(*ANTHONY just stares at her for a moment, until GLORIA motions him to speak up.*)

ANTHONY: (*Embarrassed.*) You . . . and . . . my Mom.

GLORIA: Incredible. Baby, your mom's in her seventies. She doesn't even go on to the Facebook.

ANTHONY: You're right. And if the truth be told, I see her as dead wood, but I just don't have the guts to de-friend her yet.

GLORIA: *Yet?*

ANTHONY: If mom doesn't step up her game, and get her ass in gear—she's OUT!

GLORIA: I see. So your mother's days are numbered?

ANTHONY: Just a matter of time.

GLORIA: So then, you'd be left talking with just ME?

ANTHONY: You say that like I'm some kind of loser.

GLORIA: I don't think that's the issue here. But we already live in the same house. And we already talk to each other most of the—

ANTHONY: —STOP! Gloria, would you like me to de-friend you too?! Cause if that's what you want, then so help me God, I will do it!

GLORIA: *Dios meo* . . . You would de-friend me, as well?

ANTHONY: Yes, I would. What you may not know is that de-friending these kinds of people only gets easier, after you've done it a time or two.

GLORIA: Is this not how serial killers feel about murder?

ANTHONY: What?

GLORIA: Forget it. Keep me as your friend, fine, but I still want to know what's going on with you?

ANTHONY: I already told you.

GLORIA: No, there's something else, mi Amore.

ANTHONY: Okay, then. Try this. Friends talk to each other. Friends communicate. Friends take a minute to press the damn LIKE button every once in a while.

GLORIA: Is that what this is about? You're not getting enough *likes* from your friends on the Facebook?

ANTHONY: You make it sound like nothing, but it's something.

GLORIA: Of course. I see this means a lot to you.

ANTHONY: Yes, it does. Look, when we were in Spain, you took a picture of me standing beside the sarcophagus that held the body of Christopher Columbus—inside a Spanish cathedral that was more than a thousand years old. And I think that makes for one helluva interesting photo, which is why I posted it onto my Facebook page.

GLORIA: Yes, I thought the same when I took the picture.

ANTHONY: So that makes two of us then—based upon the response I *didn't* get from everyone else.

GLORIA: Hold on a minute. As I recall, your niece wrote you back something underneath that photo.

ANTHONY: Yes, she did. "*Hey Uncle, You look like you put on a few pounds.*" That's a bullshit response!

GLORIA: So that's why you're de-friending her?

ANTHONY: Yes, it is! Think about it. Here I am- in Europe. We've never been there. And my family's never been there. Am I right? *(She nods her agreement.)* So there we were just like Lewis & Clarke going on an expedition to explore uncharted new worlds together.

GLORIA: Lewis and who?

ANTHONY: Clarke! Lewis and Clarke were a team of very famous explorers from this country.

GLORIA: They were?

ANTHONY: Forget Lewis and Clarke! The thing is that you and I were standing right beside the tomb of the guy who discovered a whole new continent. No small accomplishment, right?

GLORIA: Yes, but that guy was lying inside a black box inside of a very dark church. And I don't know if your friends could see anything in that kind of—

ANTHONY: —Don't make excuses for them. If these people want to be my friends, then they should take some interest in the life I'm living. That's all I'm saying.

GLORIA: Okay. It makes sense to me what you say, but it's just not how the world works.

ANTHONY: It's how YOUR world works.

GLORIA: *Que?* What are you saying?

ANTHONY: I see you go online every day and talk to your family- in Spain- Columbia- Chile. You message each other. You skype and tango each other- sitting at your computers in different parts of the world. It's as if you were gathered around somebody's dining room table toasting each other with a glass of wine.

GLORIA: Amore, it's what we do.

ANTHONY: I know, cause I see you doing it all the time.

GLORIA: We're Latinos, and we have a different culture. And a different mind-set about *family* then what you guys do.

ANTHONY: I don't accept that. You show me where it's written that a New York Italian family—MY family—couldn't stay connected if we wanted.

GLORIA: Sure they could. I've seen the Godfather movies. (*Smiles at him. It's a joke.*)

ANTHONY: You know what, Gloria? What you just said is *racist* and you should take that back.

GLORIA: I was just kidding. And I'm sorry for how you feel, but do you think this thing you're doing here—this *spring cleaning* is the way to get closer to them?

ANTHONY: No, but I'm trying to send a message here.

GLORIA: Right, but will your family understand that you really want more closeness with them when you push them away with the click of a button?

ANTHONY: I guess I never thought of it that way.

GLORIA: So what do you want to do?

ANTHONY: I'm confused. I mean, I just finished de-friending them. How do I take that back?

GLORIA: You can't, but you could tell them the truth about how you were feeling. Is it really such a difficult thing to do?

ANTHONY: . . . We never said what we felt in my family.

GLORIA: Which explains what you did here today, but you can still make this different.

ANTHONY: How? I already kicked all their butts off Facebook?

GLORIA: Yes, but there was a technology that was out prior to the Facebook.

(She offers him her cell phone, and he considers the phone in her hand for a moment.)

ANTHONY: No. I am *not* going to phone my brother.

GLORIA: (Beat.) ... Okay then. I guess it you will do this when you feel ready to—

ANTHONY: —I want to *skype* him. I want to see my brother's face while I'm talking to him, and telling him things I've been keeping inside for a long time. And this time I want to do it face to face, and with some respect for the guy.

GLORIA: I'm sure he will be so happy to hear from you.

ANTHONY: But I don't know how to skype. Dammit!

GLORIA: No problema, Honey. I'll teach you how to skype. In fact, I'll set up an account for you right now, but I have a request.

(She reaches for his laptop, and places it in front of herself on the table.)

ANTHONY: Sure baby, what is it?

GLORIA: Well, I don't know much about those two explorers you mentioned before. Lewis and—

ANTHONY: —Clarke. Lewis and Clarke.

GLORIA: You told me to forget them, so I did. So maybe we could call ourselves something more familiar to people nowadays.

ANTHONY: Like what?

GLORIA: Dora and Diego?

ANTHONY: Of course. I love it!

GLORIA: Sure you do. Cause it's Latin. And it's about la *familia*. So pull up a chair, Diego, right beside me, my love.

ANTHONY: You got it, Dora. Let's make this happen!

(He pulls up a chair beside her, and she begins clicking some buttons on his laptop keyboard as we . . .)

FADE LIGHTS.
END PLAY.

CENTRAL PARK WEDDING
A short play — Drama

CAST OF CHARACTERS:
BRIDE: Young Woman, Caucasian. Early-mid 20's.
STEP-MOTHER: Latina woman, mid-late 40's. Step-mother to the bride.

SETTING: Central Park, NYC. A park bench.
TIME: The Present Day. Afternoon.

Originally produced as part of **New York State of Mind—Volume III** at Actor's Workout Studio in North Hollywood, CA. Opened on October 14th, 2016.
Directed by Dolores Aguanno.

The cast was as follows:
BRIDE: Sarah Ambrosio
STEP-MOM: Maria Moreno

NOTE FROM THE AUTHOR: I would like to include a Special Thank You to Jade Anastasia who authored the POEM that is read aloud to the Step-mother by the Bride during the course of this play. Ms. Anastasia has granted this author permission to use her poem in the publishing and performing of this play. Thank you, Jade.

CENTRAL PARK WEDDING

A young BRIDE (TO BE) enters and sits down on a park bench. She's dressed in a flowing white wedding gown. An older, well-dressed Latina woman—who is the STEP-MOTHER of this bride enters now, and gracefully crosses towards this BRIDE who is seated on the bench.

STEP-MOTHER: Nina, why do you wish to talk with me now-- when your person with the camera- he wants your pictures?

BRIDE: The photographer can wait. *Escucha me, por favor.* Please come and sit with me. I need to tell you something.

STEP-MOTHER: You spoke Spanish. This must be important.

(STEP-MOTHER sits with the BRIDE.)

BRIDE: It is. I'm not feeling well.

STEP-MOTHER: You feel sick?

BRIDE: Yes. And sad.

STEP-MOTHER: Porque?!

(The BRIDE stays silent just for a moment, but continues looking at her STEP-MOTHER.)

STEP-MOTHER: You have the feet that are cold, now? In your beautiful wedding dress?

BRIDE*: (Beat.)* You loved my dad so much. I saw that. And I know he loved you, but you couldn't stay with him.

STEP-MOTHER: Your father had many problems.

BRIDE: I know. He spent money he didn't have, he smoked too much pot, and he wasn't faithful. And I don't blame you for leaving him.

STEP-MOTHER: Why do you speak of your father on this day?

BRIDE: I called to invite him, and he made up some bullshit excuse why he couldn't come. He hasn't changed, so I'm done with him!

STEP-MOTHER: I'm sorry, mi Nina.

BRIDE: You can't change anybody. I've learned that.

STEP-MOTHER: And does your Tom have problems like your father?

BRIDE: He probably should get a hobby. He never even leaves the house when I'm home, and I need my space, but I don't think that qualifies as a real problem.

STEP-MOTHER: No, it does not. And now you have invited so many people to celebrate you on this day, and they are gathering in this beautiful park- *Que lindo.*

BRIDE: It is beautiful. I'd always wanted to be married in Central Park. Ever since I saw *The Muppets Take*

Manhattan with you.

STEP-MOTHER: Yes, those Muppets were very frisky people. And the Miss Piggy has a great love for the Frog as you have for Tom, Yes?

BRIDE: Yes.

STEP-MOTHER: And we have all gathered to celebrate you in that love. And to send all these people away without giving them their prize—you must have a reason.

BRIDE: I know. I know.

STEP-MOTHER: Does he disrespect you?

BRIDE: No. He's the most respectful man I know. And he loves me more than anyone I've ever been with.

STEP-MOTHER: Then he seems like a good and decent man- *No entiendo.*

BRIDE: What if it's me?! What if he pulls the same shit with me that dad did with you? And what if he's just hiding out? What if he's on his best behavior until after we're married and then the real guy shows up and does whatever he damn well pleases like dad did with you? And if that's the way it's going to be then—

STEP-MOTHER: —But you do not know that!

BRIDE: But I know me! And I would have no patience for a liar or a cheat or a man with bad habits. And I've seen this now twice with you and my mother before you. And I know how the story ends: *"I don't like who you've become, so you go your way and I'll go mine,"* but then what's the point of marriage? Why the hell get married when it's only going to end terribly?

STEP-MOTHER: Mi Nina.

BRIDE: I don't think I'm ready to do this.

STEP-MOTHER: And what if I had not married your father? Would I have known that I had the strength to go through the problem times? And would I have ever met this sweet little girl you were? Or watch how you've grown into this strong and beautiful woman? Would I be here today with you now?

BRIDE: I guess not.

STEP-MOTHER: I have no more points than that.

BRIDE: So you're not going to give me the bull-shit that marriage is a gamble, so throw the dice, and hope for the best.

STEP-MOTHER: I don't like bets. I like to keep my money. But for you, I know that you will grow in marriage. And you will grow past this hurt that your life has given to you. And on that bet, I would place a great sum of money.

BRIDE: So you're telling me that I should just go through with it, no matter how I'm feeling?

STEP-MOTHER: That is not my decision to make, but what I could tell you is that people change. *Always* they change, and not always for the worst. Think about us. Think about how we started.

(STEP-MOTHER wraps an arm around this young BRIDE and rocks with her as if she were a young child again . . .)

BRIDE: . . . I hated you.

STEP-MOTHER: I loved you.

BRIDE: I wanted you dead. I really prayed that you would die.

STEP-MOTHER: Living with your father, there were times I prayed the same.

BRIDE: I cried a lot.

STEP-MOTHER: I wiped your tears.

BRIDE: I hid from you.

STEP-MOTHER: And I would search for you. And find you many times.

BRIDE: But I had a favorite place. And you never found me there.

STEP-MOTHER: *(Smiling.)* Your father's bathroom. You'd fall asleep in his tub.

BRIDE: But I had the curtains pulled. *(She figures it out.)* That's not even right that you never told me.

STEP-MOTHER: And there are things you will never know about yourself. Unless you try to do things, you may feel like you cannot do, but whatever you decide, I will be here for you. And when you hide, I will look for you. Even if you go and find new places to hide from me.

BRIDE: You never judged me. Not then. Not now.

STEP- MOTHER: I'd rather just love you, my baby.

(She hugs the BRIDE and looks her over from head to toe. Then recites from an old rhyme:)

STEP-MOTHER: *"Something old. Something new . . .*

BRIDE: *Something borrowed. Something blue."*

STEP-MOTHER: This is good luck. You have them all?

BRIDE: My dress is new. My shoes are blue. Could I borrow your bracelet—just till the wedding's over?

STEP-MOTHER: Yes, of course.

(She removes her bracelet and hands it to the BRIDE who puts it on her own hand.)

STEP-MOTHER: Que tiene something old?

(The BRIDE smiles, and slowly takes a folded piece of paper from inside her bra.)

BRIDE: I wrote you this poem. A very long time ago. (*She unfolds the paper in her hands.*)

STEP-MOTHER: A poem? You wrote a poem—for me?

BRIDE: Yes, I did. Right about the time you were leaving Dad. I just never got around to giving it to you.

STEP-MOTHER: You were twelve when you wrote this?

BRIDE: Uh huh. I found it the other day when I was packing up my stuff to move in with Tom. It was inside one of my old English books. Was probably too scared to give it to you then, but I'm older now, and I'm uh . . . getting married.

STEP-MOTHER: I am very curious to see this.

(*BRIDE hands the poem over to her STEP-MOTHER who begins reading silently to herself, but she stops and looks back at the BRIDE.*)

STEP-MOTHER: All these words. . . so many words. . . It would help for me to hear them in your voice. Like when you used to read those books to help me practice this crazy language of yours. Could you read your poem for me?

BRIDE: I'd love to.

(*BRIDE takes back the loose-leaf page, and reads the poem out loud to her STEP-MOTHER.*)

BRIDE: *"I hate her. I hate her accent. I hate her cooking. I hate the way my Daddy loves her. And the way she loves him back. I didn't want her around. So I told Daddy, and she backed off. And then she was gone, and I didn't expect her to do that. And I never expected to want her back. I never expected to love her. Or accidentally call her 'mom.' I never thought I'd see her again. And I never dreamt she'd be friends with my mom. I love her accent now. I love her cooking now. But mostly I love her."*

STEP-MOTHER: Nobody ever wrote for me . . . a poem of love.

BRIDE: Yes, you're right! *(Smiles)* This *is* a love poem.

STEP-MOTHER: I love you, Daughter. And I will ask for this *(re. Poem)* once this wedding is complete.

(STEP-MOTHER returns the poem to BRIDE who puts it back inside her bra.)

BRIDE: Yes, I'll keep it safe till then. I love you Mom.

STEP-MOTHER: And in this, we have not changed. No matter what you do—or where you go—or how old you become. The love remains.

PHOTOGRAPHER (OFFSTAGE) Where's the bride? We need the bride if we're going to take these DAMN photos!

BRIDE: I guess I should go back then.

STEP-MOTHER: Yes, the bride—she must be in her wedding pictures.

BRIDE: And I want to take so many pictures with you after the ceremony, so don't go anywhere.

STEP-MOTHER: Oh. I am nowhere going. *(BRIDE laughs at her words.)* Did I say that, not right?

BRIDE: No. You said it perfectly!

STEP-MOTHER: Okay then. You must go now. But know that I will be watching you and celebrating you on this, your lovely, and especial day.

BRIDE: And for you, I want you to know that I practiced this. *(With a Spanish accent that sounds similar to her STEP-MOTHER's.)* Tu siempre estaras en mi corazon.

STEP-MOTHER*: (Translating.)* "You will always be in my heart." *(She places a hand over her heart.)* Si, siempre.

(They hug once more and the BRIDE Exits. And STEP-MOTHER sits down on the bench, closes her eyes for a moment- and takes a deep breath-- as we . . .)

FADE LIGHTS.
END PLAY.

CHAPTER 2 — FRIENDSHIP

CHAPTER 2: FRIENDSHIP

Friendship has the power to change one for better or worse. All relationships that we engage in have the potential to influence us in making healthy or unhealthy choices, and perhaps this is why we've all been encouraged to *"choose your friends wisely."* Parents tend to monitor and encourage their children's friendships knowing that falling in with the wrong crowd can negatively influence their child's ability to get good grades or perhaps lead to drug and alcohol abuse, sexual diseases, and teen pregnancies (to name a few concerns).

When we look at adults with addictions, we see that oftentimes their ability to stay "clean and sober" depends upon their ability to give up old friendships or drinking buddies, and form new friendships in the various 12-step groups they attend. These new friends can encourage them on their path to sobriety. Most groups also include the option of a sponsor (mentor) who has managed to stay sober themselves over time, and will be "on call" to assist the recently sober alcoholics with the wisdom they've gathered over the years.

Winston Churchill's friendship with Franklin D. Roosevelt may have been a friendship that saved the free world during one of the darkest times in this world's history. Their frequent phone calls and letters of correspondence were filled with the warmth and trust accorded a tried and tested friendship. They provided for each other the strength and encouragement that eventually turned the tide of World War II towards the free world.

Finally, I recall the African proverb that states: "*If you want to run fast, run alone. If you want to run far, then run with a group.*" It's my personal belief—as well as a conclusion reached by considerable research—that people who have supportive and loving friendships are happier, healthier, and more productive over longer periods of time.

THE LAST CALL
A short play — Dramedy

CAST of CHARACTERS:
BOBBY: Late 30's-40's. A judgmental man. Wounded but won't admit it. Friend to Mike.
MIKE: Late 30's-40's. A patient man. A peacemaker. Friend to Bobby.
COWBOY/ GLEN: 30's. A Texan with accent to match. Alive, open, and vulnerable.

SETTING: A night-club in New York City.
TIME: The Present. About 2AM — "Last call" in a night-club.

Originally produced at Stella Adler Theatre in Hollywood, CA. as part of their **ADLER-FEST (Festival of Plays)**. Opened on February 2nd, 2018.
Directed by Kaz Matamura.

Cast as follows:
Bobby: Warren G. Hall
Mike: Sebastiano Pestoni
Glen: Kent Hatch

Also, produced as part of **Tonight's the Night—A Night of 1-Acts** at Actor's Workout Studio, in North Hollywood, CA. Opened on June 29th
Directed by Conrad Dunn.

Cast as follows:
BOBBY: Roger Gutierrez
MIKE: Paul Surace
GLEN: Greg Yoder

THE LAST CALL

Lights come up in a night-club. Two older, average looking guys, BOBBY and MIKE sit on stools that face towards the audience. They look out upon an imaginary dance floor in front of them. A half dozen empty beer bottles stand on the table beside them, and it's almost closing time. The music plays lightly in the background throughout this scene.

BOBBY: Look around this place, will ya.

MIKE: Bobby, I been looking around this friggin' dive since we got here, and now it's last call . . . Come on, man, let's go home.

BOBBY: Over there. Whatta ya see?

(BOBBY points to the middle of the dance floor where there's a lone dancer who is dancing by himself. This singular person wears Levi jeans, a cowboy hat and boots and has the general appearance of a "cowboy")

MIKE: The Cowboy? On the dance floor?

BOBBY: Right. You get the occasional guy who slips out of the herd. He dangles on the borderline betwixt heaven and hell-

(MIKE is looking at this Cowboy—studying him.)

MIKE: His shirt is open.

BOBBY: Sure. He's trying to lure a babe his way.

MIKE: But he's dancing by himself.

BOBBY: If the guy was a peacock, he'd be in full plume right now.

MIKE: Yeah. He does have his arms stretched out kinda funny. I can see that.

BOBBY: What a sorry fucking sight.

MIKE: But at least he's out there trying.

BOBBY: Ya see any ladies coming his way?

MIKE: Not one. Nobody even close to him.

BOBBY: Ya wanna do a photo essay on the *alienation* of man- then you take a picture of that guy!

MIKE: God, he *is* alone.

BOBBY: You take a video of that guy and put it on YouTube and it goes viral overnight.

MIKE: Bobby, I can't even look at the guy.

BOBBY: No! You keep looking, Mikey, cause I have a theory on what's happening here tonight.

MIKE: You gotta theory on this... *situation*?

BOBBY: You see, the guys don't like him, cause he broke from the herd. And the ladies don't like him cause he's *alone. . . isolated*—

MIKE: Like he doesn't have a friend.

(BOBBY snaps his fingers in agreement.)

BOBBY: Friendless. . . And women are always suspicious of a guy alone. It's like they're thinking—(*Spoken in a female pitch.*) *"If you can't get one of your own species to hang out with you, then what the hell do you want from me?!"*

MIKE: Maybe they think he's just here to hit on them.

BOBBY: Mike, we're all of us here to hit on them, but not like this!

MIKE: He does look wounded. Like he's not gonna make it.

BOBBY: As if it were a sin to be alone at one of these joints, but he don't know that. If you'll notice- the ladies are never alone.

(Their eyes drift over to a group of ladies who are on the dancefloor. They take in the sight of these women who are dancing together.)

MIKE: They're dancing in groups.

BOBBY: That's right! They dance in groups. They go to the bathroom in groups. And they leave in groups. As if they're afraid to meet a few eligible bachelors—such as ourselves.

(MIKE suddenly raises his beer in direction of the women on the dance floor and calls out to them.)

44

MIKE: *LADIES!!!*

(BOBBY smacks MIKE on the shoulder.)

BOBBY: Chill your ass out!

MIKE: You'd think they'd at least respect his courage.

BOBBY: Respect? Oh, Mikey, I can guarantee you it's not *respect* these women are giving to him.

MIKE: They're *mocking* the guy? Is that what you're saying to me? They're mocking this guy?

BOBBY: Mock?! That's a nice word for it. Do the words *BIG-TIME FRIGGING LOSER* mean anything to you?

MIKE: Oh Man!! That's it! This is not right. And tonight it ends! Tonight, I make it right!

BOBBY: Woah! Slow down a minute, Mikey.

MIKE: NO!!! I'm not gonna stand here and take this. I gotta do something. As *a man*—as a *brother* to that man—for the *brotherhood* of man, I've got to—I've got to bring his ass back here into the herd with the rest of us animals!!!

(MIKE stumbles forward towards the dance floor, but BOBBY wraps his arms around MIKE's waist and holds him back.)

BOBBY: Stop it, Mikey! Stop it! It's too late! Look at him.

(They both turn to look out on the dance floor—at the COWBOY—who is still dancing by himself.)

BOBBY: What kind of wretched soul ends up on a dance floor *alone* at two in the morning?

MIKE: Bobby, *we're alone* at two in the morning.

BOBBY: Yeah, but we're *not* on the dance floor.

MIKE: *(Relieved.)* That's true. And we're not alone, cause we've got each other.

BOBBY: Damn right, we do. . . You see Mikey, that guy's like a wounded animal, most probably rabid by this time, and this is why you gotta cut him loose.

MIKE: What's gonna happen to him?

(BOBBY studies the COWBOY closely for a moment and thenmakes this pronouncement.)

BOBBY: He'll dance another ten minutes by himself, making no human contact whatsoever. Then he'll wipe his bare, sweaty chest—button up his shirt—and bury his shame back at the bar with another brewskie.

MIKE: Does it have to be that way?

BOBBY: This my friend—is the cold and savage world we live in. Let's get outta here.

(They drift back to the bar as the COWBOY suddenly crosses to them. MIKE turns to catch one last look at the

COWBOY, and now sees him approaching.)

MIKE: Bobby, he's coming our way.

BOBBY: Oh shit!

MIKE: Let's just act natural.

COWBOY/GLEN: (*With a Texas accent and a smile.*) Howdy partners! How y'all doing tonight?

BOBBY: We were just leaving. Let's go Mikey.

MIKE: No, Bobby, we've got a few minutes.

GLEN: Hey that's great. Maybe I can buy you gentlemen a few beers, and we could have ourselves a get acquainted type drink together before they shut this place down. I'm Glen.

(GLEN offers his hand to BOBBY—who just leaves him hanging for a moment, until MIKE jumps in and shakes GLEN's hand.)

MIKE: I'm Mike. And this is Bobby. And the beers are on me.

(MIKE begins to exit, but first turns back to BOBBY and encourages him to shake GLEN's hand as he exits. BOBBY just stares for a moment at GLEN until. . .)

BOBBY: . . . What the hell were you thinking?!

GLEN: Not sure I comprehend what you're getting at.

BOBBY: Out there! Dancing by yourself! What the hell were you thinking?!

GLEN: If truth be told, I was thinking about my ex back in Texas.

BOBBY: You have a girlfriend?

GLEN: Had one. Actually, she was my fiancée. Past tense. She dropped me like a hot rock a few weeks back.

BOBBY: And let me ask you; did it have anything to do with your dancing?

GLEN: Hey! How'd you know that? You ain't one of them Big City psychics, are ya? I heard about them fortune tellers with their fancy Tarot cards and their big city crystal balls.

BOBBY: Far from it, but I can see what's right in front of my eyes. Look, Glen, I take no pleasure in what I'm gonna say here—

(MIKE quickly approaches with three beers in his hands.)

MIKE: Then *don't* say it, Bobby. Have a drink instead.

(MIKE hands off a beer to BOBBY. And another beer to GLEN, who clinks bottles together with MIKE. Now, MIKE tries to clink bottles with BOBBY, but BOBBY refuses his gesture and turns away from him.)

48

MIKE: Bobby and I were just saying how much we admire your courage out there on the dance floor.

GLEN: Goddamn, that's ironic. That's real damn ironic.

MIKE: Why's that?

GLEN: Cause If I'd had some real courage back in Texas, maybe me and my honey would still be together. Maybe she'd be out there dancing with me—just like we'd planned it—for our honeymoon in the Big Apple. I mean we're here in the city that don't get no rest.

MIKE: (*Correcting.*) "*Never sleeps.*" So what happened with you two?

GLEN: Ah, you guys don't want to hear my sob story.

BOBBY: You're right. Why don't we all just pack it up and—

GLEN: —She wanted me to learn one'a them crazy dances for our reception. Ya know, I think they call it the Maaca-reeena—

MIKE: (*Pronounces it correctly for him.*) Macarena.

GLEN: And I told her "*Hell no, Baby! This cowboy ain't making a fool of himself for nobody.*" And she looked at me with those big brown eyes of hers that should'a told me everything, but I comprehended nothing, cause I wasn't listening. After that, she didn't say another word.

MIKE: So you didn't want to appear foolish on the dance floor?

GLEN: That'd be an affirmative.

BOBBY: And there's nothing wrong with that.

GLEN: I thought so too, but she canceled our wedding the next day. And you know—as a man, as a prideful man—I made a decision that I will regret to the end of my days. Cause I stuck to my guns, and dug my boots in the ground, cause I was going to show her who was calling the shots in our relationship, but all I showed her was what an incredible ass I could be.

MIKE: She canceled your wedding on account of that?

GLEN: That'd be a ten-four, Amigo.

BOBBY: That smells of bullshit, Glen.

MIKE: Bobby, language please.

BOBBY: Comon, man. Let's keep it real here, Glen.

GLEN: I'm telling you the God's honest truth-

BOBBY: She dumped you over a friggin' dance?!

MIKE: Let'um talk, Bobby.

BOBBY: No way. What kinda woman does that?!

GLEN: A *mighty fine* woman who was looking for a partner, and not some "know it all" hillbilly who couldn't see that there are two sides to every story.

MIKE: Glen, you seem like a changed man.

GLEN: Yup. She took me to school all-right, but I was slow in learning my lessons.

BOBBY: Well Glen, here's a lesson for you. There's plenty of fish in the sea, but you may want to think about the kind of bait you're casting out there to lure a woman your way—

GLEN: —She was looking for the kind of man who'd be willing to take some chances and take a break from his tired old routines, and explore the world with her.

MIKE: Okay, but what about a *second* chance? People grow. People change. We're men. And we're on a learning curve, gentlemen.

BOBBY: Learning curve, my ass! I don't buy this for a minute. Call her! Call her on your cell phone! I'll talk to her for you. I'll set her straight.

(GLEN pulls out his cell-phone and stares blankly at it.)

MIKE: Bobby, there's no need for that.

(GLEN is reading from his phone now.)

GLEN: She blocked me. Changed her status on Facebook. And I got word from a buddy of mine, that she's expressed some interest in that dance instructor that was teaching her that Maaca-Reeena dance.

MIKE: (*Again, correcting him.*) —Macarena.

BOBBY: That *bitch*!!!

MIKE: *Bobby!!*

GLEN: (*Warning. To Bobby*) Woah!!! Now, you just hold your horses there, Partner! I don't appreciate that kinda language for a woman I still respect. You see, I wasn't able to give her what she wanted, but she's happy now, and I'm learning to live with that.

(**SFX:** *The song, "**Shut Up and Dance**" by Walk the Moon starts playing. GLEN stops and listens intently to the music for a moment. BOBBY and MIKE stare at GLEN.*)

GLEN: She loved this song. Dammit, I'm going back out there.

BOBBY: (*Panicked!*) Don't do it, Glen! You have no idea what you look like when you're out there alone.

MIKE: Stay with us, where you'll be *safe* with the herd.

BOBBY: Please-- Stick with the brotherhood of man!

GLEN: Sorry fellas, can't do that.

(GLEN smiles and stretches his arms out across both BOBBY and MIKE's shoulders.)

GLEN: You see, gentlemen. When I hear this song, and I dance . . . Then all of the pain, the frustration, and the bull-shit that comes from being a hard-headed man—it just melts away.

(GLEN turns from them, and begins walking out towards the dance floor . . . BOBBY and MIKE stare after him for a moment, and then BOBBY yells out.)

BOBBY: I'm going with you!

MIKE: Me too!

GLEN: I'd love your guys' company!

(MIKE crosses back to the table to retrieve the three fresh beers from off the table as he calls out to them.)

MIKE: We're pack animals you know!

*(MIKE runs after them with their three beers in hand, and exits the stage as we hear the volume rise for the song **"Shut up and Dance"** till it crescendos, as we slowly. . .)*

FADE LIGHTS.
END PLAY.

BOYS IN THE BAND
A short play — Bro-Mance

CAST OF CHARACTERS:
ROGER: A Rock & Roll Singer. Charismatic. High-school friend to Steve.
STEVE: A long time Mail-Carrier for Post Office. Nerdy. High-school friend to Roger.

SETTING: A Park Bench. In New York's Central Park.
TIME: The Present. Afternoon.

Originally produced as part of **New York State of Mind— Volume III** at Actor's Workout Studio in North Hollywood, CA. Opened on October 14th, 2016.
Directed by Paul Winfield Ehrlich.

The cast was as follows:
ROGER: Brent Harvey /Mitchell DeGuzman (alternate)
STEVE: Jessie Navarro-Parks

BOYS IN THE BAND

ROGER sits on a bench looking through his cell-phone messages while STEVE sneaks up behind him and suddenly grabs ROGER around both of his shoulders.

ROGER: Sonuvabitch! Sneaking up on me like that . . . If it isn't the Postmaster General.

STEVE: Roger "the Dodger." Long time, no see, my man!

(Awkward silence between them)

STEVE: I called. Left you like a hundred messages. You got the same number?

ROGER: Oh yeah. Number didn't change.

STEVE: Then you *did* get my messages?

ROGER: Look, Steve, I meant to call you back, but things with the band are picking up and-

STEVE: --Did you *listen* to any of the messages?

ROGER: Sure. A few.

STEVE: *A few*? Did you get the ones where Jennifer and I invited you over for dinner—like six times?!

ROGER: Dinner with Yoko? I don't think so.

STEVE: Don't call her that. Look, I know you two have never seen eye to eye, but the woman can cook. And

you've got a great dinner waiting for you if—

ROGER: —*Rain-check* on the dinner!

STEVE: Okay, no problem,. . . Thank God I finally ran into you. You know, I saw the back of your head sitting on this bench, and I could tell by the tilt—my Man, I just saw the tilt of your head, and I knew it was you! And you know why that is?

ROGER: I hadn't given that much thought—

STEVE: —Cause we got *history* together!

ROGER: Yeah. Sure. If you say so.

STEVE: Damn, we had some golden years back in high-school.

ROGER: Yeah, but then we grew up. Look, I gotta go.

(ROGER stands up from the bench. STEVE gently pushes his friend back down, and sits beside him.)

STEVE: It's bad out there, Roger, which is why they cut down our hours, let go of a ton of guys, and closed up a whole bunch of the mail stations.

ROGER: Yeah. Life's a bitch sometimes.

STEVE: Ten friggin' years delivering the mail, and now I'm just waiting for the right time to jump off this sinking ship, but enough about me, how are things with the band?

(*Another awkward beat of silence.*)

ROGER: . . . Look, I thought you knew this.

STEVE: Knew what?

ROGER: We got signed a few weeks back. We're going on the road.

STEVE: Oh my God, you gotta be kidding me!

ROGER: We signed a deal with another band that wants us to open for them.

STEVE: What band?! Shit, give me some details, my man.

ROGER: The Goo Goo Dolls—

STEVE: The Goo Goo Dolls!!! I *love* that friggin' band! Oh my God—When is this happening?

STEVE: We'll play the Garden next week.

STEVE: The garden? You mean- Madison Square Garden?!

ROGER: No, the rose garden here in the park. Of course MSG, and then we go on tour with them for the next ten months.

STEVE: This is unfriggin' believable! My God, you did it Roger. You made it happen!

ROGER: Sure, and it only took me ten years.

STEVE: Time don't matter. You did it. Hey, where was the phone call to your best buddy to fill me in on this great news?

ROGER: *Best buddy?* Look, Steve, we should probably—

STEVE: —Put me back in the band! I mean, you loved the way I played bass.

ROGER: What?! That was back in high-school! I'm working with professionals now. We got this guy on bass who toured with the Chili Peppers. *(Off Steve's awe-struck look)* That's right, the friggin' guy toured with the Chili Peppers!

STEVE: Damn, it's hard to kick that kind of guy out of the band.

ROGER: It'll *never* happen!

STEVE: You're right. Forget me playing the Bass.

ROGER: Damn straight. Look, I gotta run.

(Again, ROGER stands up to exit.)

STEVE: Where the hell are you going? We just started talking.

ROGER: Yeah, and I don't like where this conversation's going.

STEVE: Whatta you mean?

ROGER: I mean—where were you for the past decade while I was out there busting my ass!?

STEVE: I was delivering your mail.

ROGER: That's right. You took a friggin' post office job.

STEVE: Jennifer wanted me to get a *stable* job. You knew that. She wouldn't marry me unless I quit the band.

ROGER: Right. And you took that job, and you sold out your buddies. You walked away from me and the band, and never looked back.

STEVE: Jennifer made me do it! I had no choice.

ROGER: Well I'd like to advise you now- to go back to Jennifer, and get your balls back!

STEVE: You saying I got no balls?

ROGER: Exactly what I'm saying, and you gotta go back to your wife and gettum back, cause I lost respect for you as a man. And I'm playing now with guys I respect- all of whom are *manly* men.

STEVE: Now wait just a minute here. I mean, you're gonna talk to ME about being a manly man? Hell, you forgot all the porn we watched together on my father's lap-top once I stole his password? You forgot that you got laid in my Camaro while I was driving the damn thing? You gotta remember that night?!

ROGER: *(Smiling.)* It *was* a good night.

STEVE: And I hardly even turned around to look.

ROGER: That's all true. But what's your point?

STEVE: The point is—who's driving?!

ROGER: *Driving* what?!

STEVE: The tour bus! I mean you guys are going cross country, and you're gonna need a driver, right? You forgot that I drove you everywhere in my Camaro. I mean that car was a chick magnet.

ROGER: Actually, Steve, I was the chick magnet. You notice when you drove it alone that there were no chicks ever in the car.

STEVE: Yes, of course you were the chick magnet, but who was driving, man? Who was driving the damn car?!

ROGER: Steve, it was *your* car.

STEVE: Yes, and now- almost like an act of God here- I run into you at a time when you're gonna need a driver for the—

ROGER: —We've got a driver.

STEVE: You gotta driver?!!

ROGER: The guy's been driving a bus his whole life.

STEVE: Screw that guy! Who's got the history here? Some guy you never met before in your life or your old high-school buddy? I mean—Come'on Rog, if you say the word, then that guy is out and I'm in. You just gotta say the word.

ROGER: Now? *Now,* you want back in?

STEVE: Sure. I mean my feet are killing me from walking the route. Did you know I'm wearing those orthopedic shoes, and supportive hose for varicose veins that nurses wear?

ROGER: Way too much information there.

STEVE: Help a brother out, goddammit!

ROGER: You got no license to drive a bus. It ain't gonna fly, Steve, trust me.

STEVE: I'll get a license! I can make that happen!

ROGER: But even if you did, I don't call the shots anymore. You see, I got a manager now.

(STEVE is struck by the word "manager" and takes a moment to think about it. Now he begins speaking in a Rocky type of voice.)

STEVE: *"I ain't never had no manager . . ."*

ROGER: Stop it, Steve! Do not give me that scene from *Rocky.*

STEVE: *"At least you had a manager, Mick. I ain't never had no manager!"*

ROGER: This is not right—what you're doing here.

STEVE: *"Now you wanna be my manager! Go ahead, BE MY MANAGER!"*

ROGER: You rat bastard!

STEVE: We must've watched that *Rocky* DVD twenty times together, Roger, and every damn time, we both cried. No, we *wept* together during that scene. And there's no shame in that, you see cause manly men cry. So please don't talk to me about respect, and *being a man*—cause we've been there and done that.

ROGER: Look, Buddy, you got a real job. You walk away from that, and what's Jennifer gonna say then? This whole touring thing might not work out, and then where would you be?

STEVE: You're right. It might all fall apart, but you know what- It don't matter anymore- cause today . . .

(STEVE reaches down and feels for his crotch.)

STEVE: I got my balls back.

ROGER: Stop it, Steve.

STEVE: No! I swear to you. They grew back, and I can feel them now! And they're big and huge—like donkey balls.

ROGER: Stop this nonsense. Please.

STEVE: Hear me out, Roger. If you'll take me on the road with you, in *any* capacity, then I'm willing to do whatever it takes. You need a janitor to clean the toilets on the bus, then I want that job! The drummer wants his cymbals polished after each gig, then I'll do that.

ROGER: This is desperation talking, man.

STEVE: No, this is truth talking, and I'll hand in my resignation tomorrow to prove it to you. You hear me? I'll resign the post office tomorrow, and you can come with me.

ROGER: And why would you do this?

STEVE: Cause you changed me today. I swear to you, I'm a changed man, and wouldn't it be something if the boys from the band hit the road together again?

(STEVE tries to slide an arm around his old buddy ROGER, but ROGER's not having it, and moves away.)

ROGER: Yeah, that'd be something, but it's *not* gonna happen.

STEVE: Why not?!

ROGER: Cause it's too little, too late. And I got no room in my band or my bus for a sell-out.

STEVE: *Sell-out?* That was the old me. I'm changed, I'm telling you.

ROGER: Sure, I got a touring deal, and you got religion.

STEVE: Are you dumping me?

ROGER: Reality check, Steve. We outgrew each other a long time ago.

STEVE: No way. I don't think so.

ROGER: That's cause you ain't thinking in your right mind!

STEVE: Screw you, Roger!

ROGER: Screw you, Steve! And that goes double for Yoko.

STEVE: Hope your rotten tour bus crashes and burns!

ROGER: Then at least I went out like a flaming star, and not like some milk-toast delivery boy for the *puke* office.

STEVE: *(Emotional.)* You've hurt me . . . deeply.

ROGER: Look, it was YOU that came here looking for me. That tilt of my head bull-shit! You were stalking me for weeks, right? Why don't you just admit it that you were stalking me?

STEVE: Okay. Okay. I was stalking you, but just a little.

ROGER: How do you stalk someone "just a little"? What the hell- it doesn't matter. Just let it be, dammit! Don't make this harder than it has to be.

STEVE: Make what harder?

ROGER: Just get outta here, and let's pretend this didn't happen.

STEVE: And should we just *pretend* we were never friends?

ROGER: Look, I didn't come here looking for you.

STEVE: That's right. I came here looking for you—my best friend, but all I found was some ass-hole who I don't know for shit.

ROGER: That's it! I'm outta here!

(*ROGER EXITS. And STEVE'S eyes follow him till he's gone. And then STEVE lowers his head and begins whimpering like a child . . . A moment passes, and then ROGER re-enters and observes his buddy STEVE crying for a moment. And now it's ROGER who speaks in Stallone's Rocky-type voice.*)

ROGER: *"I ain't never had no manager."* Shit, that was really low bringing Stallone into the conversation like that.

STEVE: Yeah. Well friggin' Stallone made a helluva come-back after forty years, and almost won an Oscar. Me, I'm just trying to hang in there with my buddy from the band.

ROGER: Yeah, I know.

(ROGER sits down next to his buddy on the bench.)

ROGER: Look I was thinking we may need someone to do the Sound Check.

STEVE: *(In a deep voice.)* Testing. One-Two-Three. How was that?

ROGER: Not bad, but it needs a little more Basso-Profundo.

STEVE: *(In a richer, deeper voice.)* Testing. Testing. One. Two. Three.

(Tableau. A moment passes.)

ROGER: Buddy, you're back in the band!

STEVE: And the boys are back in town!

(The two friends hug—STEVE more forcefully than ROGER—as we. . .)

FADE LIGHTS.
END PLAY.

SAVING PAR
A short play — Dramedy

CAST OF CHARACTERS:
JACK: Mid 20's— 30's. A hothead. Friend to David.
DAVID: Mid 20's – 30's. Calm. Reasonable. Friend to Jack.

SETTING: A golf course. Practice putting green located within "shouting distance" of hole #1's tee-box.
TIME: Present. Morning

Originally produced as part of **New York State of Mind— Volume I** at Actor's Workout Studio in North Hollywood, CA. Opened on April 5th 2013.
Directed by Tim Simek.

The cast was as follows:
JACK: Ben Solenberger
DAVID: William Sterling

NOTE FROM THE AUTHOR: The scene that follows is a significantly revised version of the earlier "produced" scene that was performed in *New York State of Mind*- Volume 1.

SAVING PAR

JACK sits on a bench with his golf clubs standing beside him. He stares off at the first tee visibly annoyed. DAVID stands beside his bag of clubs with an iron in hand taking some warm-up practice (easy) swings as he talks.

DAVID: Wow. (*Takes a deep breath*) Nothing beats spending a day—knocking a few balls around in God's grand nature . . . The Zen of golf. (*Exhales deeply.*)

JACK: *Zen*? What the hell are you talking about *Zen*?

DAVID: Talking about what this game calls out of you. You have to be calm, focused, and relaxed to play well. It's almost like God's sending you an invitation to attend a peace party.

(DAVID follows JACK'S eyes towards the first tee.)

DAVID: Have you heard a word I've said?

JACK: Sure. God's got us going to a party.

(Both JACK and DAVID's eyes are looking at first tee box where a foursome of elderly men are gathered.)

DAVID: Why do you keep staring at those guys at the first tee?

JACK: I keep looking for their portable Oxygen tanks. Damn, how long is he just going to hover over his ball like that? Dammit.

(JACK yells in the direction of this elderly group of men.)

JACK: *Hey Pops!* You gonna hit that ball or try and hatch it?! Stop hovering!

DAVID: Hey Jack, why don't you take a few practice swings? Warm up a little.

JACK: Probably used their AARP cards for the senior discount.

DAVID: So what's it to you? Look at them. (*He gestures to the older men.*) You see them smiling, talking to each other, and laughing? You might want to take a lesson.

JACK: What the hell am I learning? (*Pointing towards one of the older men.*) You see the guy who's putting on two gloves—one for each hand? Who does that?

(*Again, JACK yells at the group at the first tee.*)

JACK: Hey, you with the two gloves, we're not doing surgery here! Hit the damn ball already!

DAVID: Would you please stop yelling at them.

JACK: Sure, if you'll stop talking about this Zen bullshit.

DAVID: Sure, if you'll chill the hell out, Bro.

JACK: Can't you see those guys are messing with my mental game?

DAVID: Yes, this is a game. And you may be mental. Yes, I *can* confirm that.

JACK: You know I don't appreciate your sense of humor right now.

DAVID: You know what this reminds me of? Last week when you missed that putt—

JACK: —Dammit! I knew you were going to bring that up.

DAVID: You missed your putt, and threw your club twenty yards towards the next hole. The guy just barely got out of the way. He wanted to say something to you, but he kept his mouth shut, cause he didn't know what else you were capable of.

JACK: Lay off man, I was having a rough game.

DAVID: No, it's more than that. Does this have anything to do with your date last night?

JACK: Why you bringing up my date?

DAVID: You called me. You told me you were excited about the date. Looking forward to the date. And now we're sitting here with time to kill, and you haven't brought up the date. Why is that?

JACK: She showed up late.

DAVID: Yes?

JACK: So I gave her a look. And she gave me a look back.

DAVID: You exchanged looks. Were they good looks, like "Hey, great to see you," kinda looks?

70

(JACK shakes his head "No.")

DAVID: Uh-huh. I think I know where this is going.

JACK: So I called her a bitch.

DAVID: You did *not* call her that.

JACK: Oh yes I did, and she gave me the finger.

DAVID: Please, stop there.

JACK: Oh no. I gave her *two* fingers back. Double pump action.

(JACK demonstrates how to give someone the "double-finger" salute.)

DAVID: Oh my God.

JACK: Date *over*.

DAVID: You called that fiasco a *date*? Think about it.

JACK: That's the problem with internet dating. They don't make matches for shit.

DAVID: The woman's a few minutes late so you curse her out, and give her the finger. No, you give her two fingers, and go home alone, and then show up today in a lousy mood. This isn't good.

JACK: Look Dave, I came here to play golf. Not to talk about my love life. *(Again, JACK looks over to the first tee.)* Is that guy using the ball-washer on the first tee?

DAVID: No, Jack, please—

JACK: *(Shouting again.)* Hey Gramps, if you really want to wash your balls, then why don't you jump into a shower with a bar of soap—

DAVID: —That's enough, Jack! I've had it with your disrespect, and you want to know something here?

JACK: Dave, please skip the—

DAVID: —I'll skip *nothing*, cause you might want to take a good look at those guys. And why is that? Cause you're looking at *yourself* in a few years, except I don't see you playing in a foursome. Not with your lousy attitude. I imagine you out here *alone* just playing with your own damn putter and balls.

JACK: Was that a masturbation reference?

DAVID: It's anything you want it to be. I'm done with you.

(DAVID hoists his bag of clubs back onto his shoulder and begins to exit.)

JACK: Don't leave me, Dave. Come on, man, let's play some golf.

DAVID: Look, Jack, I'm okay to do that, but I'm *not* okay with you coming out here and abusing the elderly.

JACK: Fine. I'll lay off them.

DAVID: We got time, Buddy. Think about it. It's a beautiful day, and time is all we got.

(Jack drops his head. He struggles to say these next words.)

JACK: That's not so.

DAVID: What do you mean?

JACK: I mean. . .my best buddy just got the diagnosis.

DAVID: Now I'm really confused, cause I thought I was your best buddy.

JACK: I'm talking about Rocky.

DAVID: Your dog?

JACK: Don't call him that. He's not just a dog to me.

DAVID: Oh man. This is tough news. What are you gonna do?

JACK: What's to do? Make his life comfortable. I don't know that I want to do the chemo treatments. He's an old guy . . . you know in dog years. He's probably as old as those guys over there.

DAVID: I didn't even know they did chemo for dogs?

JACK: Neither did I.

DAVID: I'm sorry. I had no idea.

(DAVID slips a supportive arm around his buddy's shoulder.)

JACK: What the hell. He was doing good. This came out of nowhere. Even today, His spirits are up. The poor bastard doesn't even know what's going on. And I can't explain it to him what's happening. Shit!

DAVID: You can talk to him. Maybe he'll understand your energy. They're smart like that.

JACK: I had that talk with him. He was laying down on the rug- all stretched out and getting some sun. And I got down on my knees and was just looking at him for a minute, and then he turned his face to me and looked at me with those big brown eyes of his. And he started to lick me in the face. Ya know those are kisses, right? The guy's giving me kisses while I'm telling him that his life's coming to an end. That just kills me, man.

DAVID: That's beautiful.

JACK: You know what's beautiful? The guy sleeps with me in the bed.

DAVID: Yeah?

JACK: I shut off my light. And that's the signal between us. He comes and lays his body right up against my pillow and I put my hand around his chubby little belly, and you know what he does?

DAVID: No idea.

JACK: He takes his paw and puts it over my hand. It's like we're holding hands together. That kills me, man.

DAVID: That's beautiful.

JACK: I mean that's true love. *(Thinking. Then quickly.)* Dave, please don't mention this to any of our friends.

DAVID: Sure.

JACK: You know, I've had some girlfriends who told me they wouldn't sleep with me, if Rocky was gonna sleep in the bed with us.

DAVID: And what'd you tell them?

JACK: *"Don't make me choose."*

DAVID: Makes sense. Look Jack, maybe today's not a great day for golf. Maybe we should just go grab a bite to eat or something.

JACK: No. Rocky's sleeping. He sleeps most of the day. And I want to play a game of golf with my friend.

DAVID: Sure Buddy. If that's what you want. Then let's do it.

JACK: What I like about this game is you get to talk while you play.

DAVID: Sure, so why don't you tell me some more about Rocky.

JACK: No, I want to tell you about last week, when we were out here and I threw my club. You remember when you hit that lousy tee shot that rolled off the fairway behind a row of trees?

DAVID: Sure. The green's about a hundred yards away but I'm stuck with a row of trees standing in front of my ball.

JACK: They were *really* tall trees. And I watched you, and I was looking for you to panic or struggle with your next shot, but you didn't tip your hat. You just reached into your bag, pulled out a hybrid and without so much as a practice swing, launch the ball low and way to the left of the trees. And then it starts fading to the right. The ball speed is good as it curves past the trees, a beautiful arc through the fairway, so that it curves around and rolls all the way onto the green.

DAVID: Yeah, a fade comes in pretty handy at times.

JACK: No, it was more than that. That shot spoke to me.

DAVID: It did?

JACK: You didn't try and force it through the trees. Or go over the top of them. And you didn't play it safe, and just lay it out there onto the fairway. You just went the hell around them, and damn if you didn't save par in a situation where I thought it was hopeless. And it moved me. It touched me. Damn, I sound like a friggin' loser here.

DAVID: Nah, You sound like a guy who's getting in touch with some deep feelings. And that's okay, Jack, it's okay.

JACK: That you could make that kind of shot in such a peaceful way. It was like God was talking to me, telling me that things were gonna be okay. And in that moment, I was happy.

DAVID: You were. I saw the smile on your face, and you gave me a high-five, but the very next hole, you missed a putt, threw your club, and told me you had to leave. What happened, Bro?

JACK: I think . . . uh . . . this thing with Rocky. It's like I got a tree standing in front of me now, and this tree's blocking out the sun, and leaving me in a darkness where it's cold, and I got no light to see my next shot. I don't see the green anymore. Is it dogleg right or left? Is the stick planted in the middle, back, or front of the green? All these things, I'm clueless. I don't have a damn idea in my head on how to proceed with my next shot. And I don't have your fade so that I know things are going to turn out all-right. I don't have that shot in my toolbox. And I know I have to face this thing but. . .

DAVID: You're looking for a shot.

JACK: And I don't have it! I don't have the shot I need to save the little guy.

DAVID: You still have to play it, Bro. And you gotta play it as it lays. And the shot will come, and whatever it is, it'll be *your* shot. And it will be the *right* shot.

JACK: You think so?

(DAVID puts a hand on JACK'S shoulder.)

DAVID: I know so. And I'm here for you, man. I'm standing with you.

JACK: Yeah, I see that now.

(These two friends look at each other, and debate whether to hug one another. They exchange smiles instead, until JACK looks again towards the first tee.)

JACK: Looks like we're all clear now.

DAVID: Then let's play this game.

JACK: For sure. . . *(Calmly exhaling.)* The zen of golf.

(These two friends hoist their bags onto their shoulders, and exit the stage, crossing towards the first tee as we. . .)

FADE LIGHTS.
END PLAY.

WAITING FOR BUSCEMI'S CALL
A short play — Dramedy

CAST OF CHARACTERS:
DONNY: Long time Mailman. Close friend to Bob since high school. Had big dreams of Hollywood glory.
BOB: Long time Mailman. Close friend of Bobby's since High school. More of a follower.

SETTING: Bob's Apartment.
TIME: Around Christmas. The present.

Originally produced as part of *New York State of Mind—Volume II* at Actor's Workout Studio in North Hollywood, CA. Opened on June 6th, 2014.
Directed by Paul Storiale.

Cast was as follows:
DONNY: Paul Surace
BOB: Robert DiTillio

NOTE FROM THE AUTHOR: *This play is the one exception to my earlier statement that all the characters in the plays are fictitious. Obviously, the well-known actor Steve Buscemi is a real person. I attended high school with him, shared an acting class, and performed in a play with him during that time. Although we were not good friends, I recall Steve as a kind-hearted, generous, and funny young man, as I've been told he remains so today, even with his celebrity status. I have the utmost respect for him and what he has accomplished as a Film and TV actor, writer, producer, family man, and loyal friend to his inner circle and extended family. Also note that the situation depicted in this scene is made up and never happened. In no way is it my intention to be dismissive or poke fun at Steve's celebrity and/or lifestyle, but rather my intention is to comment on the nature of friendship and disappointed dreams.*

WAITING FOR BUSCEMI'S CALL

BOB is seated at a kitchen table inside his small, Long Island apartment that is decorated with several Christmas type ornaments. He stares at his land-line phone which sits in the center of the table. DONNY sits across from BOB who stares at him. Now, BOB gestures with both his hands stretched out towards the phone, as if he's encouraging the phone to ring.

BOB: Ring, damn phone! RING!

DONNY: Take it easy, Bobby, let's not jinx this.

(Both men stare at the phone, and appear as if they were a "mirror image" of each other. A moment passes, and then)

DONNY: Will you stop looking at the phone!

BOB: You're looking, too.

DONNY: You're right. Let's stop this right now.

BOB: Stop what? What's to stop?

DONNY: Are we losers that have nothing better to do then stand around and wait on a call from Steve Buscemi?

BOB: Hell no, Donny! We are not losers!

DONNY: Which is precisely why I'm suggesting we walk away.

BOB: Walk away? From what?

DONNY: The phone. Let's turn ourselves around. And walk away.

BOB: So we should walk around and just clear our heads a little? Is that what you're suggesting?

DONNY: Absolutely! Is it me, or is Buscemi playing mind games with us?

BOB: Mind games, Donny? I don't follow.

DONNY: You don't follow? Really? We wrote this awesome script for Steve that we've been sitting on for years. And then we just so happen to bump into the guy while we're doing our Christmas shopping . . . There HE is. There WE are. And you don't follow?

BOB: I don't follow.

DONNY: Bob, the stars are finally lining up for us here, and you don't follow?

BOB: Buscemi's a star. I *follow* him. These other stars you're talking about; I'm not following.

DONNY: So you don't follow that if we got our script to Buscemi, then everything changes for us?

BOB: Donny, I think that—

(Suddenly, DONNY pounds on the table, and stands up from his chair.)

DONNY: Get away from the phone *now*!

81

(*BOB also stands up from his chair. And together they begin walking away from the phone. However, both continue to stare over their shoulders towards the phone- while they continue walking until **SFX:** PHONE RINGS LOUDLY!!!*)

BOTH: Shit, it's him!!!

(*They both turn, and make a mad dash to pick up the phone, but in doing so, they collide with each other and tumble to the floor and the phone with them. DONNY who's lying prostrate on the floor, snatches up the phone from the floor, and yells loudly into the receiver.*)

DONNY: *Hello?! Hello?! Who is this?! Who is this?!* . . . Sonuvabitch! He hung up on me.

BOB: Why would he do that?

DONNY: He sensed it.

BOB: Sensed what?

DONNY: The desperation. Did you see us? Falling all over ourselves to pick up the damn phone.

BOB: Yes, we did. But Donny, his guy called us this morning, and left us that message to call him back.

DONNY: *His guy?*

BOB: You know, his assistant.

DONNY: Mr. Fancy Dancy! Steve has an *assistant* call his two best buds from the neighborhood? You see what I'm talking about?

BOB: No, I don't. Buscemi's a busy guy.

DONNY: He's also a powerful guy who doesn't want to talk to weaklings.

BOB: He doesn't?

DONNY: Of course not! We lost sight of who we are.

BOB: We did?! *(Beat.)* Who are we, Donny?

DONNY: We're *men*, goddammit!

BOB: I agree. Yes, we *are* men.

DONNY: Grown men. Who do not depend upon the kindness of strangers, or friends, to survive. It's NOT who we are, Bob. However, if the guy wants to do us a favor, and I want to be straight up about this—if Buscemi wants to help us out in this matter, then it is not for us to refuse an offer of kindness from a friend. And we won't refuse it. However, if he just wants to dick us around-

BOB: *Dick us around?*

DONNY: Then the conversation will NOT go well.

BOB: Not *well*? It won't go *well*? So you think we should call him and find out?

DONNY: Absolutely not! I refuse to engage in this power-play bullshit!

BOB: Whatta ya mean power-play?

DONNY: I mean who's the alpha dog here? We don't play that shit.

BOB: No way are we playing that shit! *(Thinking.) Alpha dog?*

DONNY: I don't give a rat's ass who the guy is.

BOB: Sure Donny, but we're talking about our long lost buddy from the neighborhood. We were the *Three Amigos* back then, and our *amigo* said we should call him.

DONNY: My God! I'd completely forgotten about the *Three Amigos*. We sat together every day at that same lunch table.

BOB: Sure Donny, and he gave us his number.

(BOB pulls a scrap of paper from his pants pocket, and waves it at DONNY.)

BOB: Here it is, and he said we should—

DONNY: —You couldn't pull the three of us apart with a crowbar. We were so close.

(Observing DONNY who's still lost in his reveries, BOB puts the scrap of paper back into his pants pocket.)

BOB: Sure, I remember that. You remember how you'd give Buscemi your chocolate milk?

DONNY: Of course! The guy loved chocolate milk! Couldn't get enough of it, and if the guy wanted my lunch, I gave it to him, no questions asked. There was even that one time, he offered to pay me for it. And I looked him dead in the eye and said: *"No charge for an amigo."*— but we let our amigo slip away.

BOB: Sure, Donny. We graduated, and got our jobs with the Post Office, but Steve, he moves into the city and starts working with the Fire Department.

DONNY: And then he starts acting in those strange little plays in the Village. Remember? We went to see him a few times.

BOB: I never understood what those plays were about. Every time I thought Steve was saying something serious, the people around us was cracking up. And then when I was laughing, they were serious. It was like what the hell's going on here?!

DONNY: They were confusing, but the guy was out there learning his craft, and it was then that it first hit me. *(Beat.)* The *Three Amigos* were no more.

BOB: Yeah, but we could always see him in his movies. I mean, there he was—our high school buddy- right up there on the big screen.

DONNY: Buscemi *rockets* to stardom, and we're left standing around with our hands on our mail sacks...

delivering the goddamn mail. But we all had a dream back then.

BOB: And our buddy did it! Like he won the lottery or something, and Donny, it wasn't so long ago that he was just another guy from school. Like one of us.

DONNY: You're right. And when we ran into him on the street, it was like no time had passed. We were cracking wise together, all of us reliving old times like the guy didn't want to leave. Must've been a good thirty minutes that we just stood there talking.

BOB: It was *two* minutes, Donny. I timed it. Before he tells us he has to go.

DONNY: Two minutes? Bullshit! I swear he looked like he was choking up when he tells us he has to go.

BOB: He wasn't choking up, Donny. He had a cough. I don't think he looked well at all.

DONNY: That's bullshit! I looked into his eyes, and I swear the guy was tearing up on us.

BOB: Those weren't tears, Donny. The guy had a cold or allergies, cause he blew his nose a few times also.

DONNY: You're out of your mind! *Busce* was in *great* shape that day.

BOB: He didn't ask one question about us. A minute goes by, and he tells us he's in a rush to get someplace. Me personally, I thought he was giving us the bum's rush!

DONNY: That's a lie! He tells us how great it was seeing us. And that's why he goes for my idea to exchange phone numbers right there in the middle of the street.

BOB: That's true. He did give us his number, and said we should call him, so why don't we just—

(BOB again moves to pick up the phone, but DONNY puts his hand directly on top of the phone so that BOB cannot pick it up.)

DONNY: The guy don't even know that you and I wrote a script together with him in mind for the lead.

BOB: How could he know that, Donny, when he didn't ask one question about us?

DONNY: Will you stop with your negativity! Buscemi's gonna love our script, and you know why? Cause we put things into our script that only close personal friends would know.

BOB: Sure, like we know his favorite color is *yellow.*

DONNY: Right! So our script opens with Buscemi driving over the Brooklyn bridge- in a *yellow* Camaro.

BOB: While he's eating a lemon!

DONNY: Exactly! We grab them by the balls right up front with intimate, personal details like that.

BOB: But he ran away from us so quick, we couldn't tell him nothing.

87

DONNY: Bob . . .Bobby. . . Bobby boy . . . Sit down for a minute.

(DONNY sits his friend BOB down on the couch, and then sits himself beside him.)

DONNY: You see Bob . . . the man has performed with all of the great stars in a lot of movies. He starred in an HBO series with none-other than Mr. Martin Scorsese producing, and before that he gave James Gandolfini a massage on The Soprano's and then tried to kill the guy—*who does that?*

BOB: Our buddy Steve does.

DONNY: Right, but not only does he act, he also directs, and he even wrote a few scripts on his own that got made into movies. So when you got that kind of success happening to you, you're always in a rush to get somewhere. *Gabeesh*?!

BOB: I guess so, Donny, but like you said, maybe he's home for the Holidays and still wants to hook up with his old crew from the neighborhood.

DONNY: Of course, he does.

BOB: Okay then, I'll just call him now, and get the party started.

(BOB stands up, and puts his hand on the phone. Now, DONNY stands up and gives him a warning look. Tableau.)

DONNY: You'll do nothing of the sort.

BOB: What are you saying?

DONNY: You got a friend like Buscemi, who's got the *juice* to do you a favor in Hollywood, you never call that kinda guy!

BOB: What?! Isn't that the point? The guy's connected. We're asking him to read our script. Is that too much to ask?

(BOB picks up the phone.)

DONNY: Put down the phone, Bob.

BOB: What is friendship about, if you can't ask for a teeny, tiny. . .

(DONNY snatches the phone from BOB's hand, and slams the receiver down into the cradle.)

DONNY: We're not calling.

DONNY: When he calls us, then we'll ask. And even if he reads our script, and don't like it, it doesn't matter.

BOB: *It doesn't matter?*

DONNY: You see we're confident we wrote an excellent script. So we don't take it personal if Steve's not impressed, cause then we just ask him to pass it along to some of his Hollywood friends so they can read it.

BOB: *Pass it along?*

DONNY: An *introduction*, Bob. We simply ask Steve for an introduction.

BOB: An *introduction?*

DONNY: To *introduce*. . . the act of introducing. To meet others in show business we could not meet on our own.

BOB: I get it. He's successful. He's running in circles we're not.

DONNY: Of course, the man's *running in circles*.

BOB: And we're not in those circles, Donny, but he could introduce us—just like you said.

DONNY: Sure, and then we could all be running in circles together. A lot of circular running, Bob.

BOB: I see. So I guess we'll just have to wait around and see if Buscemi calls.

DONNY: And when he does, we kiss the frigging post office good-bye! But the guy has to pick up the damn phone and call us.

(SFX: of PHONE RINGING AGAIN—LOUDLY.)

BOTH: It's HIM!!!

(BOB reaches for the phone, but DONNY slaps his hand away.)

DONNY: Don't pick up!

BOB: Why not?!

DONNY: We're not desperate. Not like before. Let it ring. *(Phone rings for second time.)*

BOB: It's ringing.

DONNY: I hear it ringing.

(Phone rings for third time.)

BOB: It rang, Donny. The phone, it rang again.

DONNY: So let's pick it up, cause it's GO time!

(DONNY picks up the phone, and yells loudly into the receiver.)

DONNY: Hey Stevie boy! How the hell are you?! . . . *MOM?!* What the hell?! I told you not to call today, and that we were waiting on a very important call . . . Yes! I'll bring home the quart of milk. I didn't forget, now hang up the damn phone! Mom, we can't continue this conversation. . . I've got to go. Mom, we need to hang up now. *(DONNY slams the phone down into the cradle.)* Dammit! I've got to move out of my mother's house. She doesn't respect my space!

BOB: I don't like this, Donny. I don't like this situation at all.

DONNY: It's a damn shame what's going on here. Buscemi's messing with my mind!

BOB: That's it. Screw it. I'm calling the guy.

DONNY: Are we desperate, Bobby? I think not.

BOB: Donny, we should do this.

DONNY: Are we weaklings, Bobby? I think not.

BOB: I don't care how it makes us look. We know who we are, Donny.

DONNY: Are we not *men*, Bobby?

BOB: Sure, we're POST-men! Who deliver the mail. And we're always gonna be postmen unless Buscemi does us a favor and reads our script. So what's the big deal? We are who we are. And if we want to ask an old friend for a favor, and this makes us look desperate or weak, then so be it. He gave us his damn number *(BOB again pulls out scrap of paper, and holds it out to DONNY.)* And I'm calling this number, cause that's what he asked us to do. You hear me, Donny?! That's what our friend—No, our *amigo*—has asked us to do. And I'm doing it!

DONNY: You are one weak, Sonuvabitch.

BOB: Screw you, Donny! I'm not so weak that I can't pick up this phone, and call a friend.

(BOB begins dialing.)

BOB: I'm calling.

DONNY: I see you calling. And it's breaking my heart over here.

BOB: Quiet! *(Listening to the phone.)* It's ringing. The phone's ringing. (*BOB raises his head to the heavens, and closes his eyes.)* Pick it up. Dear God, pick up the phone!

DONNY: Buscemi will *not* pick up his phone.

BOB: You're wrong. A friend would pick up the phone.

DONNY: Yeah, but he's a star now, and those kinda guys all turn their backs on the people they grew up with.

BOB: I don't believe that. It stopped ringing. *(BOB presses the phone closer to his ear.)* Hello? Hello? . . . Yes, this is Bobby uh . . . Robert Dubrow. And I'm calling for Steve . . . uh . . . Steve Buscemi. He told us to call this number . . . Did you say that he was *expecting* our call? . . . You'll put me right through? To Steve? ... Thank you! Thank you very much!

DONNY: He's bringing Steve to the phone?!

(BOB nods "Yes" to DONNY, and speaks into the phone.)

BOB: Steve is that you?! . . . Oh fantastic. Great talking to you again. Yeah, I'm doing great. And I got Donny right here by my side-

(DONNY snatches the phone out of BOB's hand.)

DONNY: Stevie Boy, it's Donny! How are you doing mi amigo?. . . Me and Bob, we were talking, but nothing

93

about you. Just shooting the shit with each other like in the old times, but then Bobby starts fiddling around in his pocket, and I told him that he should stop playing "pocket pool" with his balls—ya know—*(DONNY cracks himself up.)*

BOB: Would you tell him about the script?

DONNY: But then Bob pulls out the piece of paper with your number on it. And you know how life gets crazy cause we completely *forgot* we had your number. And I say to Bobby, *"Whatta ya say we give Busce a call?"*

BOB: Please Donny, tell him about our script.

DONNY: Sure, Steve. I know you're a busy guy. It's the holidays. Who isn't busy right? But in remembrance of what once was, me and Bob wanna invite you out for a drink, and just like in the old times, the *Three Amigos* will close down the bar, and ride off into the sunset once more. . .The *Three Amigos*, Steve! You gotta remember the *Three Amigos*. . .You have no memory whatsoever of the—

BOB: —Get to the point already, Donny. The script!

DONNY: An offer for drinks is still on the table, Steve, and your high school buddies are buying- *"No charge for an amigo."* . . . An AMIGO, Steve! Goddammit—an AMIGO!

BOB: Would you cut the *amigo* bull-shit, and give me back the phone!

(BOB snatches the phone back from DONNY, and speaks calmly into the phone.)

94

BOB: Hey Steve, it's Bob here again, and we'd really like a chance to sit down and talk with you ASAP, maybe even tonight if possible.

DONNY: We just need an introduction.

BOB: *(Into phone and to DONNY also.)* You're taping a special tonight? With Robert DeNiro and Al Pacino? . . . You three guys are doing a Christmas show together?

DONNY: Screw *those* three guys! What about the *Three Amigos!?*

BOB: *(Into phone.)* You want my address?

DONNY: Yes! He wants to visit us when he's done taping his show.

BOB: *(Into phone.)* You want to put us on your Christmas card list?

DONNY: Christmas Cards? What the hell?!

BOB: *(Into phone. No emotion.)* Sure, Steve. Christmas cards are nice.

DONNY: We need *introductions,* not Christmas cards!

BOB: *(Into phone.)* Sure, buddy. We'll talk to you soon.

(DONNY snatches the phone back from BOB, and speaks into the phone rapidly, and with great desperation now.)

DONNY: Steve, it's Donny! And we wrote a script for you, and we'd like for you to read the damn thing. . . Who is this?! . . . Steve's assistant? What the hell! Could you put Steve back on the line?! . . . He's stepped out already? . . . You want my address? For a Christmas card?

BOB: Just hang up the phone, Donny.

DONNY: *(Into phone.)* Yeah, I'll get back to you with that.

(DONNY hangs up the phone, and the two amigos stare at each other for a moment. Both exhausted by the call.)

BOB: . . . He told us to call.

DONNY: And we did as we were told.

BOB: So we did the right thing, then?

DONNY: Who's to say, Bob? I'm totally goddamn bewildered right now.

(DONNY sinks down into the chair at the kitchen table with head in his hands. BOB observes his dejected friend for a moment.)

BOB: You want a beer, Donny?

DONNY*:* Nah, I gotta get home to my mom, with that damn quart of milk.

(DONNY stands up and crosses towards the door, and suddenly turns back around to his friend.)

DONNY: Hey Bob, would you call me tonight with that number? I wouldn't mind getting a card from Buscemi, cause as much as we've told those *morons* at the P.O. how close we were with Buscemi, they still look at us like we're bull-shitting them.

BOB: I noticed that. They kinda give us that dumb look whenever we bring the guy up in conversation, but a Christmas card from Steve would act as proof that—

DONNY: —*Absolute* proof! And the card would come to us thru the mail right while we're sorting it, and we just open it up and pull out the card, and show it to them.

(DONNY holds his hand up in the air as if he were displaying the card.)

DONNY: Hah! Try and deny this, you *Bitches!*

BOB: And won't they feel like real frigging morons when we show it to them.

(BOB now mimics his friend, and holds up his hand as if he were displaying the imaginary card to his post office buddies.)

BOB: What's this I got over here in my hand, *Bitches*?!

DONNY: He may even write something to us. A few words- special like- into the card.

BOB: I seriously think it could happen. I mean think about it. Steve friggin' Buscemi—*movie star*—picked up the phone and talked to us today.

DONNY: He did that . . . Man, that'd sure be something. *(DONNY turns to exit and takes a few steps towards the door.)*

BOB: Hey Donny.

(DONNY turns back to his friend.)

BOB: Merry Christmas, mi amigo.

DONNY: Yeah . . . Merry Christmas, mi amigo.

*(DONNY crosses to BOB and gives his "amigo" a great big bear hug. Then he begins to exit the apartment when once again **SFX: PHONE RINGS LOUDLY!***

Both DONNY and BOB turn and stare at the phone, but this time, DONNY just shakes his head, and continues to exit the room. BOB also ignores the phone as it continues ringing, and sits down at the table, examines the scrap of paper in his hand . . . as we . . .)

FADE LIGHTS.
END PLAY.

Photos from the Plays — HEARING VOICES

From *Boys in the Band* with Brent Harvey and Jessie Navarro-Parks (pg. 54)

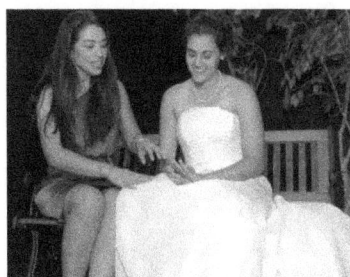

From *Central Park Wedding* with Maria Moreno and Sarah Ambrosio (pg. 27)

From *Finding Faith* with Devin Caldarone and Allegra Williams (pg. 107)

From *Father's Day* with Greg Yoder and Paula LaFayette (pg. 5)

From *The Last Call* with Paul Surace and Roger Gutierrez. (pg. 41)

From *Toda La Noche* with Paula Lafayette and Danny Christenson (pg. 123)

From *Waiting for Buscemi's Call* with Paul Surace and Robert DiTillio (pg. 79)

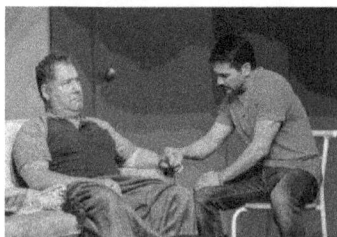

From *Saying Goodbye* with Paul Surace and Holger Moncada, Jr. (pg. 212)

Photos from the Plays — HEARING VOICES

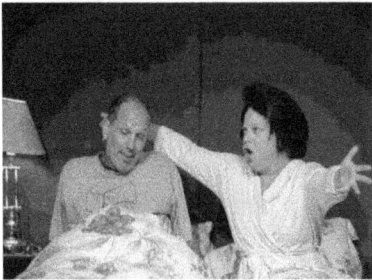

From *One Night in Elvis* with Cliff Weissman and Jylian Sy (pg.137)

From *The Misery of Hope* with Tony DeCarlo, Patricia Canale, and John-Paul Lavoisier (pg. 191)

From *Saving Par* with William Sterling and Ben Solenberger (pg. 67)

From *Fakebook Friends* with Ana Valverde and Justin Bryant Rapp (pg. 15)

Photos from the Plays — HEARING VOICES

From *Glory Days* with Ronnie Rose and Julie Dolan (pg. 161)

From *Grave Knowledge* with Chris Karmiol and Catherine Mersereau (pg. 170)

The author of HEARING VOICES, Paul Richard Surace

Rocky, co-star of three of the plays from HEARING VOICES

CHAPTER 3 — LOVE

CHAPTER 3: LOVE

For most people, there's nothing more frightening then trying to create and nurture a love relationship. It's difficult trying to negotiate the stark differences between two unique personalities and their different physical and emotional needs. The key word in the above sentence is "negotiate" for there may be arguments and disagreements between couples that aren't solvable. However, that doesn't mean they have to break up—as long as they're willing to "make the *problem* the problem and not the *other person* the problem." That ability to *make the problem, the problem* is the key to having successful negotiations between differing parties. It asks that each party be respectful of each other's differences, and thus allows each to feel no less loved while they try to come to a compromise or negotiation between them. If two parties can stay respectful and not make each other out to be the enemy or "adversary" when they fight, then they are in a better position to stay connected and problem-solve their way through whatever challenges or issues come up.

The Bible says: "*Greater love hath no man than this, that a man lay down his life for his friends.*" (John 15:13) And many Christians relate this to be a spiritual message of Christ's willingness to lay down his own life in order to purchase salvation freely for his followers. I can also see how this verse applies to love relationships in general as it probably explains why it is that military men who have fought in combat together, and are literally willing to die for one another on the battlefield, are able to create such deep and loving bonds of friendship that are rarely matched in civilian life. It may also explain why marital researcher and psychologist, John Gottman, states that it is basically a respectful "friendship" that will keep marriages together, and serve as a vital antidote to divorce. One can observe that in a healthy marriage or committed partnership, the individuals must be willing to "lay down their lives" (figuratively speaking) and be willing to make great sacrifices on behalf of their partner—during both the good and the bad times—so that the two will grow to become a healthier, happier couple.

FINDING FAITH
A short play — Romantic Comedy

CAST OF CHARACTERS:
BOBBY FALCONE. Mid-Late 20's. Brooklyn native. Sensitive. Lost and vulnerable since recent breakup with Faith.
FAITH. Mid-late 20's. Brooklyn native. No nonsense type of gal. Loves Bobby, but is confused by his behavior.

SETTING: Brooklyn, New York. Bobby's Apartment
TIME: THE PRESENT. AFTERNOON.

Originally produced at Actor's Workout Studio as part of **New York State of Mind—Volume I** in North Hollywood, CA. Opened on April 5th, 2013.
Directed by: Paul Surace

Cast was as follows:
BOBBY: Chris Guerrero
FAITH: Emma Travis

NOTE FROM THE AUTHOR: A *significantly* revised version of the original play was produced again as part of **New York State of Mind—Volume** III at Actor's Workout Studio in North Hollywood, CA. Opened on October 14th, 2016.
Directed by Conrad Dunn.

Cast was as follows:
BOBBY: Devin Caldarone
FAITH: Allegra Williams

FINDING FAITH

BOBBY sits on his living room couch wearing frumpy—even bizarre looking—pajamas. He wears stereo headphones over his ears, and leans forward as he's copying things down from a book onto index cards that are spread out on the coffee table in front of the couch.

BOBBY: Yes, I will do this!

(Loud knocking on the door but BOBBY doesn't hear it through his headphones. More loud knocking on the door, but BOBBY continues writing things down onto the index cards. **SFX: A key jiggles in the door's lock**. And door opens revealing an attractive young woman named FAITH who enters the apartment. She crosses towards BOBBY who is not aware of her presence. She's directly behind him now, as he continues scribbling onto the index cards.)

BOBBY: My God, this is awesome!

(Now, FAITH removes the headphones from BOBBY's ears. Surprised, he turns back to see her, and they lock eyes for a moment.)

FAITH: Hello, Bobby. Nice to know you're still alive.

BOBBY: Hello, Faith.

FAITH: I called a bunch of times but it went straight to voice mail.

BOBBY: Yeah, I been having a problem with my phone.

FAITH: Well then, I guess it was good that I came over, so we could talk in person, face to face like.

BOBBY: What are you doing here?

FAITH: What's the matter, Bobby? You look frightened to see me.

(She points to all the index cards and the book laid out on coffee table.)

FAITH: What's going on here?!

(BOBBY quickly picks up the book from the coffee table, as if to protect it. FAITH grabs a handful of the index cards, and looks through them quickly, but is confused by them, so she flings them back onto the table.)

BOBBY: Hey, be careful with my stuff.

FAITH: What the hell are you doing here?

BOBBY: I'm reading. I'm writing.

FAITH: What are you reading? *(She snatches the book from him, and reads the title out loud.)* "2001 Things to Do Before You Die"? Why are you reading this?

(BOBBY snatches the book back from her. He holds the book up to her.)

BOBBY: This is a great book! It's got wisdom I never even thought about.

FAITH: If you say so. And what are you listening to? *(Now, she puts his headphones over her own ears to listen to the music he'd been listening to.)* *"Live Like You're Dying"*? You don't even like country music.

BOBBY: Well, I like it now! These people from the country tell great stories. And some of them are very inspirational.

(Now, FAITH notices his bizarre looking pajamas.)

FAITH: What are you wearing? Is this a joke?

BOBBY: It's no joke, Faith!

FAITH: And where are your New York Knicks boxers you wore to bed with me? The sexy ones. Where are they?

BOBBY: I threw them out. Basketball's for suckers. I got more important things to do with my life. And I see now, that you breaking up with me was all for my good.

FAITH: Is that what you see? Because what I see is you wearing some very *loud* pajamas, and it's the middle of the day, and you don't even wear pajamas.

BOBBY: Well, I'm wearing them now!

FAITH: Why do you keep yelling at me?

BOBBY: Maybe cause you interrupted me in the middle of doing something that was very important.

FAITH: Yeah, like reading books about death? And listening to songs about death? So tell me how this is important for you.

BOBBY: Cause I'm studying, and I'm making plans.

FAITH: What kind of plans? You haven't purchased any weapons, have you?

BOBBY: Not *those* kind of plans. Plans about my life. Plans about my future. I wrote some things down on these cards. I'll read one to you if you'd like.

(FAITH simply stares at him. BOBBY lifts an index card off the table, and begins reading from the card.)

BOBBY: *I will keep an aquarium.*

FAITH: An aquarium? Ya know you're really creeping me out here. I'm calling your mother. Where's your cell phone?

BOBBY: I don't have it.

FAITH: Why not?

BOBBY: I threw it away.

FAITH: And why would you do that?

BOBBY: Cause it was mocking me.

FAITH*:* Mocking you? Your phone was mocking you?!

BOBBY: I swear to God. It was laughing at me. Tormenting me to make a decision about our relationship that I had no power to make. *(Begins talking in a strange voice.)* *"Call her, Bobby, and beg her to take you back, but you don't deserve her cause you're a moron!"* Over and over. So I finally had enough, and threw it out the window. And when it hit the ground, and smashed into so many tiny little pieces, then I started laughing!

FAITH: How was that funny?

BOBBY: Cause it was ME, who had mocked the phone!

FAITH: So how do you plan on talking to your friends or me?

BOBBY: There's no need to, cause now I'm talking to myself! *(She laughs at him.)* Seriously, Faith, I'm having conversations with some really deep places inside myself. Places I didn't even know existed.

FAITH: So you're having conversations with yourself? *(Suddenly frightened.)* Oh My God, you're hearing voices!

BOBBY: Just one. My own! The voice of Bobby Falcone. And you wanna know something really sad?

FAITH: Sadder then what I've already heard? I don't see how that's possible.

BOBBY: Oh it's possible. Cause this voice of mine, I almost didn't recognize it, but now that I've spent some time alone. En-communicado. I see that it's the only voice worth hearing, and I finally got the ears to hear it!

FAITH: And none of this seems strange to you?

BOBBY: More like *transcendent*.

FAITH: *(Suspicious.)* That's a big word. One I never heard you use before.

BOBBY: Well I'm using it now! Cause I'm reading more, increasing my vocabulary, and my understanding of things. And you wanna know something. . . I really thought you'd be happy for me.

FAITH: How can I be happy when you're like this? What happened to the Bobby I knew? The guy who loves basketball, is always talking to his friends, and playing Candy Crush on your phone, which you broke.

BOBBY: I'm a different person now.

FAITH: Yes, you're *deranged* now, but I had no idea that our breaking up would do this to you, but we can change things between us—

BOBBY: —*We'll change nothing!* I feel like a man on fire where all my senses have been magnetized and sensitized and enlarged-a-size. Do you know that last night, I sat and listened to the shower faucet drip into the tub for six hours straight?

FAITH: I told you to fix that leak!

113

BOBBY: *I'll fix nothing!* It was magnificent! I could hardly wait for the next drop to drip.

FAITH: Did you sleep at all last night?

BOBBY: Who needs sleep when you've found *tranquility*?

FAITH: *(Suspicious.)* Another big word. And they both begin with the letter "T" *(FAITH is suspicious, and starts looking around the apartment for something.)*

BOBBY: You gotta problem with big words?

(FAITH's eyes land upon a large book sitting on the couch. She picks up a Dictionary, and opens it to where the bookmark is situated inside.)

FAITH: Interesting how it's bookmarked at the letter "T." Have you been studying from the back of the Dictionary?

(BOBBY snatches the Dictionary from her, and throws it down on coffee table.)

BOBBY: You *do* gotta problem with *big words!*

FAITH: No, I don't, but I have problem with you being sleep deprived. What about food? Have you been eating?

BOBBY: I had a grape yesterday.

FAITH: A grape?!

BOBBY: Might've been an olive. Not sure really.

FAITH: That's it! I'm going to fix you something to eat.

(FAITH exits into the kitchen.)

BOBBY: NO! Don't open the—

*(From off-stage, we hear **SFX: of many books crashing onto the floor.**)*

FAITH (Offstage): BOOKS!

(She re-enters crossing to BOBBY.)

FAITH: Your kitchen cabinets are filled with books!

BOBBY: I'm feeding my soul.

FAITH: Oh my God, when does this end? Aren't you hungry?

BOBBY: For *wisdom*, Yes.

FAITH: Bobby, you're a plumber from Brooklyn, and you're sounding bat-shit crazy here. That's it. I'm dialing 9-1-1. *(She pulls out her cell phone.)*

BOBBY: No! No! You put away your phone and listen to me now.

(She hesitates, but returns her phone back into her pocket.)

BOBBY: Ya know the first couple of days without you were unbearable. I kept pacing the floor like some kind of caged animal. I felt lost, confused, frightened. Like I was dying inside, and it was then that I'd realized I'd lost my faith, and that's when I fell to my knees and prayed like hell to get it back again.

FAITH: Well Halleluja! Cause your prayers have been answered.

(FAITH makes a gesture as if to say: "Here I am!")

BOBBY: Not you, Faith. The other kind of faith where you hope that things can change for the better.

FAITH: And how's that going? Cause from the looks of things here —

BOBBY: —You know that plan I told you about, that I wanted to build an aquarium? You never asked me why I'd wanna do something like that.

FAITH: What the hell does an aquarium have to do with our future?

BOBBY: Nothing and *everything*!

FAITH: The more you talk, the more confused I get.

BOBBY: Fish. . .

FAITH: Are we playing password here?

BOBBY: How do fish live their lives?

FAITH: Wet?

BOBBY: No! They don't stress. And you wanna know why?

FAITH: Cause they have teeny, tiny fish brains?

BOBBY: False! I reject that!

FAITH: And how do you know they don't stress?

BOBBY: Cause I've done the research! Yesterday, I went down to Vinny's Jungle Aquarium on the corner, and I stood there for hours just staring at the fish in his tanks. That was until Vinny threw me out, saying I was bad for business, but not before I figured it out.

FAITH: Figured what out?

BOBBY: Those fish were talking to me!

FAITH: Talking fish? This sounds familiar. Like a DVD movie we recently saw together-

BOBBY: Leave DORY out of this!

FAITH: I'm just saying those fish had problems.

BOBBY: I reject that! Don't feed me that Hollywood bullshit of what a fish is thinking, cause they ain't thinking about nothing, and you're missing the point.

FAITH: Okay then. I'm gonna stop myself, and listen to you. Cause if you've got a point to all of this stuff I'm seeing, then I wanna hear it. *(FAITH sits down on the couch.)* Come here. Come sit with me. *(BOBBY sits down beside her.)*

BOBBY: I want to grow up. I want to be a better man.

FAITH: I like that Bobby. I really like that. And it honors me that you'd want to do that for me.

BOBBY: Not for you, Faith. This is for *me*. For Bobby Falcone.

FAITH: Even better. And I tried telling you when we broke up that I wanted something deeper with you. Remember? I told you that I wanted a boyfriend who could make our relationship a priority.

BOBBY: I want that now too.

FAITH: And have you got any ideas on how to do it? I mean it's great that you're reading books, improving your vocabulary, and listening to country music, but I'm just not sure how that helps us.

BOBBY: That's where the fish come in!

FAITH: Oh man, we're back to the damn fish?!

BOBBY: Those fish I saw at Vinny's were like little Zen Buddhist Monks with puckered lips telling me about the power of *now*!

FAITH: The power of now?

BOBBY: You see fish don't think ahead and get all worried about the future. And they don't go backwards in their mind, and hold onto memories of all the bad things that ever happened to them which would only get them depressed. Thus, they live their lives in the present moment- every moment—ya see? And that's the power of now.

FAITH: And how does this apply to us?

BOBBY: Oh man, you still don't get it.

FAITH: But I'm listening cause I want to get it. So go on.

BOBBY: I've always been the guy wrapped up inside my skull who's thinking ahead and expecting the worst things to happen.

FAITH: You feel that way about us too?

BOBBY: Sure. What if we marry, and I lose my job? Or we marry, and I gotta low sperm count and we can't have kids? Or we marry, and you . . . stop loving me?

FAITH: Oh Bobby—

BOBBY: —I don't think I could live through that kind of thing again. These last few weeks have been—

(FAITH puts a hand over his mouth to silence him, and whispers these next words sweetly to him.)

FAITH: And what if we marry, and live happily ever after?

BOBBY: But there's no sure way we could predict that.

119

FAITH: You're right. And from what you just told me, you would only be predicting the worst things to happen.

BOBBY: That's probably right.

FAITH: Bobby, do you think you may have a chemical imbalance?

BOBBY: That's probably right too.

FAITH: You know there are pills you can take for that.

BOBBY: Yeah, but I want to do more than just shove a few pillsdown my throat. I want to change some stuff up here.

(He takes his finger and points to his head. BEAT. She takes his same finger, and moves it down so it now rests over his heart.)

FAITH: And maybe here too?

BOBBY: Yeah.

FAITH: And I think this idea that the fish gave to you about not thinking too far ahead is a good one.

BOBBY: You do?

FAITH: Sure! And having some kind of faith that things can change for the better—that sounds very positive to me.

BOBBY: And maybe it'd help some if I started talking to a shrink?

FAITH: I wouldn't stop you.

BOBBY: And what if I go ahead and build an aquarium?

FAITH: Why not? You know what I love about you, Bobby? You're a guy who's willing to try new things.

BOBBY: Yeah, I do that.

FAITH: Which is why I'd like to try and grow old with you.

BOBBY: You'd want to spend the rest of your life with me?

FAITH: I want to, Bobby, I really do. But we'd have to take it one day at a time—ya know, kinda like the fish, and see how it goes.

BOBBY: That'd give me some time to grow up a little.

FAITH: Sure. And me too.

BOBBY: Awesome. That way we could both study the fish in the aquarium I build, and master the power of now.

FAITH: Okay. But you know what I'm feeling at this present moment?

BOBBY: No idea.

FAITH: I'm feeling that I should show you the power of *right* now.

(She kisses him passionately for a moment, and they break the kiss.)

BOBBY: Oh boy.

FAITH: But you'll have to lose those frumpy pajamas.

BOBBY: Oh, I can do that.

(She smiles and offers him her hand. He takes it, as they begin crossing to exit to the bedroom.)

FAITH: Did you seriously throw out your Knicks boxers?

FADE LIGHTS.
END PLAY.

TODA LA NOCHE
A short play — Romantic Comedy

CAST OF CHARACTERS:
MATTHEW: A young man in his mid to late 20's thru 30's. Logical. Still trying to find his footing with his young Latina bride. Married to SOPHIA.
SOPHIA: A young and attractive Latina woman in her mid to late 20's thru 30's. A "firecracker" who is passionate, funny, and married to MATTHEW.

SETTING: A small apartment.
TIME: The present.

Originally produced as part of *In the Bedroom — A Night of 1-acts* at the Actor's Workout Studio in North Hollywood, CA. Opened on May 5th 2017.
Directed by Dolores Aguanno.

The cast was as follows:
MATTHEW: Danny Christenson
SOPHIA: Paula LaFayette

TODA LA NOCHE

MATTHEW and SOPHIA lie in their bed together, and they stare at each other, just after a very "intimate" encounter has taken place between them . . .

SOPHIA: That was the most romantic and passionate love we made, tonight, my baby. And now, I'm going to hold you *toda la noche.*

MATTHEW: Sweety, you always want to hold me *toda la noche.*

SOPHIA: If that's a crime, then call 911.
(And she wraps her arms around him tightly.)

MATTHEW: I don't think we need to get the police involved, but you know when you hold me like this, I get very warm.

SOPHIA: You mean like *hot*? For me?

MATTHEW: No, like smothered. Like I can't breathe.

SOPHIA: That doesn't sound good.

MATTHEW: It's not.

(He gets up from the bed, turns on the standing floor fan, and then jumps back into bed.)

SOPHIA: *(Coughs.)* Baby, you know the fan makes me cough.

(She jumps out of bed, turns off the fan, and then jumps back into bed with him.)

MATTHEW: Okay then. How about some fresh air?

(He doesn't wait for an answer, but jumps out of bed, and opens the bedroom window, and then jumps back into the bed with Sophia.)

SOPHIA: Honey, it's cold outside, and you know I get a rash when the weather's like this.

MATTHEW: You know I forgot about that.

SOPHIA: How can you forget something like that?

(She jumps out of bed, and closes the window, and then jumps back into bed with Matthew.)

SOPHIA: Now turn around and let me hold you *toda la noche*.

(He stays in place looking at her. Beat.)

MATTHEW: You asked me a question.

SOPHIA: I did?

MATTHEW: You asked me how I could forget something like the cold weather giving you rashes on your face. And I wanted to answer that for you.

SOPHIA: Please do.

MATTHEW: Well Sophia, before you came into my life, I'd never met a woman who was *allergic* to the cold.

SOPHIA: Yes, I am a very uncommon woman. And you've seen the rashes I get on my face, and you know that's not too sexy. *(She goes to kiss him, but he turns away from her.)*

MATTHEW: Yes, I agree. Not too sexy.
(He picks up the TV remote, and turns on the TV.)

SOPHIA: What are you doing?

MATTHEW: What does it look like I'm doing?
(He watches TV, and sets the remote down on the bed.)

SOPHIA: You know I can't fall asleep with the TV on.
(She picks up the remote and suddenly clicks off the TV.)

MATTHEW: Hey, Jimmy Kimmel's doing his monologue.
(He reaches to get back the remote from her, but she holds it away from him.)

MATTHEW: Hey, give that back!

SOPHIA: *(Flirtatious.)* You want it, then you can have it, but you will first have to give me *muchos besos*.

MATTHEW: Forget it. You can keep it. Maybe I'll just read.
(He picks up a book from the nightstand, and opens it to read while she studies him.)

SOPHIA: What is the matter with you?

MATTHEW: Look Sophia, you just vetoed me on the fan, the window, and the TV, and yet you seem to think it's perfectly okay for you to hold me *toda la noche*?

SOPHIA: But we made the love, and now it's time to sleep.

MATTHEW: But I'm not tired. And I really wanted to watch TV.

SOPHIA: But I have read the books about sleep, and they say you're only supposed to use the bed for sleeping and making the love.

MATTHEW: Well, I'm glad that all of the experts agree on that, but it seems that you forgot to consult with me about it. And I also happen to be a sleep expert myself.

SOPHIA: Really?

MATTHEW: Oh yeah. Been doing it since I was a baby.

SOPHIA: Very funny. Okay then, my darling Matthew, I will listen to you now, not only with my ears, but *con mi corazon tambien*.

MATTHEW: Why are you bringing your heart into this? Really, I'm fine with just your ears.

SOPHIA: You are a cranky boy tonight.

MATTHEW: Yes, I am.

SOPHIA: Well please explain. *Habla porfavor.*

MATTHEW: Sophia, do you know that before you came into my life, I used to love falling asleep with the TV on? And that it calmed me down, and helped me to fall asleep?

SOPHIA: What are you saying?

MATTHEW: I'm saying that all the things I used to do in my bedroom at night—like breathe some fresh air, or watch some TV, or even to stretch out my arms which I cannot do when you're holding onto me so tight that it's like I'm in a straight-jacket.

SOPHIA: What is this jacket that is straight?

MATTHEW: It means I can't move when you're holding me so tight, and I can't do any of those other things. They're done, and gone forever!

SOPHIA: My god, you are so dramatic.

MATTHEW: Is it drama or my sad reality?

SOPHIA: Sad? Why are you sad? Look at what you have gained for yourself. *(SOPHIA makes a big gesture referring to herself.)*

MATTHEW: Is there some kind of rule where I can't have a wife, and still watch TV in my bedroom?

SOPHIA: Yes, but not when it's time to sleep. And I appreciate the *sacrifices* you have made for me, so now you can tell me my dear husband, what can I do for you? Can I scratch your back? Or give you a big, juicy good-night kiss? *(She goes to kiss him, but he refuses.)*

MATTHEW: No kissing. We're talking here.

SOPHIA: Is there some kind of rule you've made where we cannot kiss while we talk?

MATTHEW: Look, maybe I should start sleeping in the living room where I could leave the balcony door open for fresh air, and watch TV till I fall asleep.

SOPHIA: But then we could not fall asleep *together*.

MATTHEW: Right. But I have a plan already made in my mind—that once you fall asleep in here then I can tip-toe back into the bedroom, and get into the bed, but ever so gently, so I don't wake you up. And then I can sleep right next to you for the whole rest of the night, just like you want. Now that's a really good plan, huh?

SOPHIA: That plan *sucks!*

MATTHEW: Why?

SOPHIA: Because then I can't hold you while I'm still awake. Did you know that when I hold you in the bed, it's the most beautiful thing in the world? It is the thing that I most look forward to at the end of my day. And it puts me into the most peaceful sleep.

MATTHEW: Maybe you should try Melatonin.

SOPHIA: *I want you!* And I don't even hold you *toda la noche*. I hardly even hold you *media* noche.

MATTHEW: You know what babe . . . *media* noche . . . a *quarter* of the noche! *Nada* la noche! You're missing my point.

SOPHIA: *(Translating "quarter" for him.)* That would be said *quarto* de Noche.

MATTHEW: Whatever! It doesn't make it right or cute, just because you can say it in Spanish.

SOPHIA: I have an idea.

MATTHEW: Ideas are good.

SOPHIA: If you want the air that is fresh—

MATTHEW: —Fresh air, yes.

SOPHIA: Then maybe you could take a walk outside just before you come to bed.

MATTHEW: Okay. That sounds good. Maybe we could take that walk together. What do you think?

SOPHIA: It would be too cold for me, but you could walk with Rocky.

MATTHEW: Rocky?!

SOPHIA: Sure. It will give him another chance to poop before he goes to bed.

MATTHEW: Did you just give me one more chore to do?

SOPHIA: Okay, Forget walking Rocky. I'm just trying to fix this problema. Have you got any ideas, Mr. Wise-man?

MATTHEW: Yeah, stop giving me chores to do.

SOPHIA: Seriously. Some ideas, por favor?

MATTHEW: How about earplugs? If you wear earplugs, then the TV won't bother you.

SOPHIA: Sweety, you know that earplugs—

BOTH: —hurt my ears.

MATTHEW: Dammit! Do you hear yourself?

(She reacts strongly to his cursing.)

SOPHIA: Why do you curse at me? And why is your squawking TV box so important to you? Do you not understand the *treasure* you have found in me? Because if you do not understand that, and if you take me for granite-

MATTHEW: —That's *granted*, not granite.

SOPHIA: What?

MATTHEW: Take you for granted. You said *granite* which is like a hard rock.

SOPHIA: Which is like your head! And you are being mean to me, and I don't like it. And if you want to watch your damn TV so much, then you go and take your damn TV and you put your damn TV way up inside your ass, cause I'm leaving now! *(She turns from him and begins to exit.)*

MATTHEW: No! Sophia, don't go—

SOPHIA: No, you should really watch your TV. Jimmy Kimmel has a good *monogram* he's doing.

MATTHEW: It's Jimmy Fallon, and it's a monologue. Look I want you to stay. I'm sorry that I cursed.

(She stops and turns to listen to him.)

MATTHEW: The point is. . . do I get to say *no* to you?

SOPHIA: Of course!

MATTHEW: Not so quick. Hear me out, please. You are this warm, loving, passionate creature, and you smother me with love almost all the time and you know what?! It's too darn much some time. And I don't even deserve it some of the time.

SOPHIA: *(Correcting.) Most* of the time, you do not deserve this love of mine.

MATTHEW: And you know what else? It's hard to tell you no—so I say *yes* to you—when I really want to say *no*, and that's not right cause every man has the right to say *no* to his wife no matter how beautiful and loving she is.

(She is touched by his speech.)

SOPHIA: *Que linda!* Matthew, you melt my heart when you speak like this.

MATTHEW: Hold on a minute, did you hear the part about me saying no to you?

SOPHIA: Yes. And you can say no to me.

MATTHEW: But will you take no for an answer?

SOPHIA: Of course! *Most* of the time.

MATTHEW: Aha! Most of the time- sounds like you just gave yourself a pass there.

SOPHIA: Yes, cause there are some things in life that really deserve a yes.

MATTHEW: And just how do we determine that?

SOPHIA: How important is it to the person we love? Cause love makes sacrifices, Honey.

MATTHEW: *Sacrifice* is an interesting word, Sophia, but why does it seem like I'm the only one here making any sacrifices?

SOPHIA: Really? You feel that way with me?

MATTHEW: Look Babe, in this situation—I'm making ALL the sacrifices here.

SOPHIA: . . . . That's right. You're right.

MATTHEW: And in a partnership, we both have rights.

SOPHIA: That's right too.

MATTHEW: Good. I'm glad we're both seeing things the same way here, partner. *(He smiles at her, and she smiles back at him— a big smile.)*

SOPHIA: . . .So then you tell me, *Partner*, where are you when I'm doing your laundry and folding your clothes into the drawers? Where's my *partner*—when I'm cleaning your bathroom, or cooking your meals at night after I come home from a full day of work? Where's my *partner* when I'm every day keeping our home clean and organized? Cause it's at those times—that I feel that I have no partner but am making all the sacrifices for the man that I love.

MATTHEW: I didn't know you felt that way.

SOPHIA: I do. But I don't really, cause I love you, Honey. And I want you happy.

MATTHEW: I know that, but you never brought those things up till now.

SOPHIA: Cause I do them for you. For us. To make our home a place of peace and love. I don't just want to tell you how much I love you; I want to show you how much I love you, and this life we've created together.

MATTHEW: I hate it when you do that.

SOPHIA: Do what?

MATTHEW: Make more sense than me.

SOPHIA: No, I'm glad you spoke to me about this. I want you to be happy with me, and if holding you *toda la noche* is making you unhappy then I can change that for you.

MATTHEW: You would do that?

SOPHIA: Yes, I would. And you want to know why?

MATTHEW: Sure.

SOPHIA: Cause I want to hold you close to me—*toda mi vida.*

MATTHEW: *(Translates her words).* "All my life." Damn, what am I going to do with you?

SOPHIA: Just love me, and as for you watching TV at night in the bed, I've seen that they have those headphones with no wires, that use the *weefee* to connect to the TV. Maybe we could both of us live with that.

MATTHEW: Yes, I think that would work. Okay then. You want ideas, then I've got one too. You can hold me at night until you fall sleep. And then after that, I'd need some space to breathe again. Would that work for you?

SOPHIA: Oh yes! Just like a sleeping pill.

MATTHEW: I love you, Baby.

SOPHIA: And I love you, mi esposo.

(And she goes to kiss him, and this time, they do kiss a lovely kiss. . . as we . . .)

FADE LIGHTS.
END PLAY.

ONE NIGHT IN ELVIS
A short play — Romantic Comedy

CAST OF CHARACTERS:
DOMINICK: An overweight and balding middle-aged man. A former Elvis impersonator who now feels depressed and lost. Married to Margaret.
MARGARET: A middle aged woman. A former Elvis impersonator. Acts and looks younger than her age. Sexy and loving towards her husband, Dominick.

SETTING: A Hotel Room in Las Vegas
TIME: The present. Late Night.

Originally produced as part of *In the Bedroom — A Night of 1-acts*. At the Actor's Workout Studio in North Hollywood, CA. Opened on May 5th, 2017.
Directed by Conrad Dunn.

The cast was as follows:
DOMINICK: Cliff Weissman
MARGARET: Jylian Sy

ONE NIGHT IN ELVIS

It is late night in a Las Vegas hotel as an overweight, middle-aged man named DOMINICK sits on the bed changing the channels on the TV. There's a picture of a young, sexy Elvis Presley that sits in a prominent position within this room. His attractive middle aged wife, MARGARET, enters wearing sexy pajamas and an Elvis wig that appears to resemble Elvis's famous pompadour from his early days. DOMINICK moves his gaze from the TV to his wife.

DOMINICK: Hey babe. What's with the pompadour?

MARGARET: I'm getting ready for the convention tomorrow.

DOMINICK: Right, but the convention's *tomorrow*, and I'm not interested in sleeping with Elvis tonight.

MARGARET: Honey, *what happens in Vegas, stays in Vegas.*

DOMINICK: Elvis was a good looking guy, but I was hoping to sleep with my wife tonight.

MARGARET: Sleep? (*Sexy smile.*) I was hoping for more than just sleep.

DOMINICK: Then you'd better lose the wig.

MARGARET: It took me forty minutes to get it right –

(He ignores her, and goes to remove it, but she slaps his hands away.)

MARGARET: Leave it! Com'on baby, once we turn off the lights, the hair won't get in the way. Ya know I'm feeling. . . *(Sings the Elvis lyric.)* **"Lonesome Tonight."**

(She shuts off the lights, and the room goes dark. MARGARET moves towards the bed.)

MARGARET: Maybe I'm channeling the King tonight.

(The room suddenly lights up. DOMINICK stands by the light switch he's just turned on.)

DOMINICK: Seriously?

MARGARET: What is your problem?! I've never seen you like this.

DOMINICK: And I've never seen you like this, when we're about to make love, and it's freaking me out.

MARGARET: Baby, have you never heard of role-play? *(Sings the Elvis lyric.)* **"It's now or never…"**

DOMINICK: Yes, I have and if you came out here with a short skirt, and a feather duster in hand, then count me in, but you're playing Elvis. I mean this is sacrilege.

MARGARET: Sure it is. IF you still worship at the altar of the King, but I'm not sure anymore.

DOMINICK: Baby, baby, baby. We met at the Viva Las Vegas Convention.

MARGARET: Ten years to the day... *(Sings the Elvis lyric.)* **"Viva Las Vegas"**

DOMINICK: And who could've guessed that we'd both be wearing the same outfit—

BOTH: *(Remembering)* The powder blue jumpsuit with gold sequins.

MARGARET: Or choose to sing the same Elvis song that night.

BOTH: *(Both sing the Elvis lyric.)* **"Hunk of hunk of burning love."**

DOMINICK: And later that night, at the good-bye party, we gyrated our hips against one another (Elvis Style) while we danced to a Deejay playing a medley of his greatest hits. *(Sings the Elvis lyric.)* **"One night with you—is all I'm praying for . . ."**

MARGARET: It was as if Elvis had ordained for us to find each other. And we married in that cute little Vegas chapel later that weekend.

DOMINICK: Hell, we even had Elvis there performing the wedding.

MARGARET: *(Correcting.)* A guy dressed like Elvis. And baby, tonight, on our anniversary, I wanted to *bring back the magic.*

DOMINICK: What do you mean?

MARGARET: I mean . . . your powder blue jumpsuit has been hanging in your closet for years now. And the silky silver scarf with it.

DOMINICK: I know that.

MARGARET: But what troubles me most—is that your pompadour sits atop some lifeless mannequin's head—alone and neglected for years. Talk about *sacrilege.*

DOMINICK: Margie, those days are over.

MARGARET: Are they, Dominick?

DOMINICK: I can't wear that stuff anymore. Look at me. *(He places his hands on his large belly)* I wouldn't do the King proud.

MARGARET: Elvis put on weight.

DOMINICK: Baby, that was Elvis in the age of *decline.*

MARGARET: He was *still* Elvis.

DOMINICK: I will not portray him like that. The man deserves to be remembered the way he was—like a Greek god in powder blue spandex.

MARGARET: Baby, are you talking about Elvis? Or *yourself*?

(DOMINICK remains silent.)

MARGARET: I thought so. . .Honey, It's been years that I've left this alone, but I think it's time now that you came to terms with this *thing* that's happened to you.

DOMINICK: What *thing*? What are you saying?

MARGARET: Baby, I brought along your pompadour. It's here with us tonight.

DOMINICK: You did not!

MARGARET: Yes, I did.

DOMINICK: And why'd you do that?

(She puts one finger to her lips to quiet him. Then hands him a cardboard box that holds a mannequin's head with his pompadour wig set on top of it. He carefully lifts up the head so that just the pompadour wig can be seen above the top of thebox. He stares at it for a moment.)

DOMINICK: My goodness... the hair's blacker then I remembered.

(He touches the wig carefully, gently stroking the hair with great tenderness and love.)

MARGARET: I want you to wear it tonight while you. . . *(Singing the Elvis lyric.)* **"Love me tender... love me sweet."**

(Suddenly, he drops the mannequin head with wig back into the box, and moves away from it, as if he can no longer be in its presence.)

DOMINICK: Baby, I can't. . .

MARGARET: *(Singing Elvis's lyric)* "**When I feel like this, and I want to kiss, don't say can't. . .**"

DOMINICK: Please stop singing, Margie. I can't put it on.

(She crosses to him and holds him in her arms.)

MARGARET: Oh yes you can, Honey. So what that you're overweight; Elvis was overweight. And so what that your hair has thinned out; why do you think Elvis changed his hairstyle so many times over the years? And so what that you get out of bed three times a night to pee; Elvis's last moments—God rest his soul—were inside a bathroom at the foot of a toilet so he knows where you're going thru.

(She goes to kiss him, but he turns away.)

DOMINICK: You don't understand. Baby, I was the guy that stood up on that stage and made it happen! You talk about *magic*. I swiveled my hips, and all the pretty girls fell down in a row. *I felt. . . so powerful* back then.

MARGARET: Look Dom, It makes sense that you'd miss that kind of power to have all the little chickadees fainting at the sight of you, and I could give you a pep talk about the one woman who didn't fall at your feet, but instead stood proudly by your side in that chapel to recite her marriage vows. And who's standing in front of you now, but I'll save that speech for another day.

DOMINICK: Good, cause I got it, babe. I know that I won the lottery when you came into my life, but let me ask you something. Would you have given me a second lookback then, if I looked like I do now?

MARGARET: I don't know how to answer that, but I do know that I accept what you've become, and if you can do the same, Dominick, then you just might be able to take back your power, and feel the magic again.

DOMINICK: I'll give that some thought.

MARGARET: You do that. You think about it, and while you're at it, why don't you think about the *man* who brought us together. The *man* we both love and adore. . . the *man* who taught us all how to age—not gracefully—NO, he did not, but he lived long enough to show us that no matter what you look like, you can still go out there and *wow them* right till the very end. And I submit to you—my beloved husband–that this was what his final years were all about, and maybe yours, too.

DOMINICK: I never thought about it like that.

MARGARET: I know. And I think if this Man among Men, if he were here with us tonight. . .

(She goes to Elvis's picture and picks it up for a moment to admire it).

MARGARET: And who's to say he isn't? Then he'd want you to wear his pomp—especially tonight.

DOMINICK: You think so?

MARGARET: Yes, and that's a bet I'd let you make here in Vegas.

(They both look at the picture of Elvis now for a moment, and then DOMINICK slowly lifts his old Elvis wig from the box and places it on his head, but it doesn't quite fit right, so MARGARET adjusts it for him.)

DOMINICK: How do I look?

MARGARET: Just like the man I fell in love with.

DOMINICK: It's been a long time.

(He goes to a mirror and takes a look at himself, runs his hands thru the wig, smiles at himself, and sings this Elvis lyric to himself in the mirror.)

DOMINICK: *"Well it's one for the money—Two for the show—Three to get ready— GO CAT GO!"* *(Turns to his wife)* Baby, this feels good.

MARGARET: Of course it does.

(She walks towards the bed, pulls the covers down, and lies seductively atop the bedsheets.)

MARGARET: Honey, I think I'm getting—*(Sings the Elvis Lyric.)* *"**All shook up. . . "***

DOMINICK: Your hips feel like moving?

MARGARET: Sure do. With the man I love. Why don't you turn out the lights and come to bed... *(In an Elvis type voice:)* **my hunka, hunka burning love. . .**

(DOMINICK sees the look of desire on his wife's face, and then his body language changes – so that he suddenly has a swagger to him.)

DOMINICK: Wow, I feel something good happening... *(Looks down towards his crotch area)* almost *magical* happening-- right about now.

MARGARET: Yes, the King Lives on. Now, come to bed.

(He smiles, and turns off the light switch, and crawls into bed beside her. They hold each other for a tender moment, until we hear these next words in a deep Elvis type voice.)

DOMINICK: *"Thank you. Thank you very much."*

(SFX: ELVIS's classic song: BURNING LOVE *plays overhead now—* as we --)

FADE LIGHTS.
END PLAY.

BLIND-SIGHT
A short play — Romantic Comedy

Cast of Characters:
PETER: Husband to Naomi.
NAOMI: Wife to Peter. Anxious about eye surgery about to happen.

SETTING: This couple's apartment.
TIME: The present. Morning.

NOTE FROM THE AUTHOR: This play has not yet been produced.

BLIND-SIGHT

NAOMI and PETER sit across from one another at a breakfast table. They are nicely dressed and each have a cup of coffee in front of them.

NAOMI: I can't see you.

PETER: (*Taking her hand*) I'm right here.

NAOMI: I know you're there. I can hear that you're there, but I can't see you.

PETER: Babe, you really can't see my face?

NAOMI: None of your features. You're a blur.

PETER: Wow. I don't think I've ever been referred to as a *blur* before.

NAOMI: I looked in the mirror, and I couldn't see my own face either.

PETER: No worries there. You're looking lovely as usual, my dear, but why are you panicking when you haven't put in your contacts yet?

NAOMI: Even with them in, my vision is worse now than it's ever been. You forgot that I failed the DMV vision test twice before I passed it?

PETER: I didn't forget, but third time was a charm.

NAOMI: What if I hadn't passed it?

PETER: Why are you bringing that up when you passed it already?

NAOMI: What if I couldn't drive, what would my life be like?

PETER: You could always get around with Uber.

NAOMI: I don't like Uber.

PETER: All-right then, Lyft. You like Lyft.

NAOMI: You're missing the point. I want to get in my own damn car and drive wherever the hell I want to go.

PETER: You passed, Naomi. Let it go, would you.

NAOMI: *(Frustrated. Standing up.)* My eyes suck.

PETER: Right, which is why we're getting you *new* eyes. The first one today *(Looking at his watch)* in about two hours.

NAOMI: *We're* not getting new eyes. *I'm* getting new eyes—*only me*, and I don't want to do this cornea transplant.

PETER: Yes, you do. We did all the things we needed to do to get you ready for this. And now you go forward today, and you'll have a brand spanking new cornea that will eventually let you see twenty-twenty.

NAOMI: They didn't guarantee twenty-twenty.

PETER: Right, but whatever you get: twenty-thirty, twenty-forty, it'll be better than what you've got now.

NAOMI: And what if my eye rejects it?

PETER: That won't happen.

NAOMI: It happens all the time. They're going to scrape off my cornea and paste some stranger's cornea in place of my own, and keep their fingers crossed that my eye accepts it.

PETER: And it will, 'cause this new laser technology is great!

NAOMI: Sure, he'll take that laser, and cut zig-zag lines into my eyeball so the new cornea can grab hold of what's left of mine.

PETER: Yessir, that's why they call it cutting edge technology.

NAOMI: How about I *cut* some zig-zag lines in *your* eyeball and see how much you like it.

PETER: Ya know, in the old days, it would take an old fashioned miracle to make the blind to see again. You realize you're doing this now, without getting Jesus involved.

NAOMI: I've told you not to bring Jesus into our conversations when I'm upset.

PETER: *(Looking upward.)* Forgive her Lord, for she knows not what she says.

NAOMI: And what if the person who donates the cornea is a *criminal?*

PETER: What?

NAOMI: You heard me. What if I get the eyes of a kidnapper or a bank robber? Oh my God, what if it's a *murderer* who donates his cornea to me?!

PETER: Woah! Slow down a minute. They don't do that kind of thing.

NAOMI: Criminals can't donate their organs?

PETER: I hadn't really thought about it.

NAOMI: Well, I have. And what if I get this *wicked* person's eyes, and I start doing *wicked* things, 'cause I'm seeing the world thru his *wicked* eyes.

PETER: That sounds like a Twilight Zone episode.

NAOMI: Seriously, what if I suddenly develop a fascination for guns or knives?

PETER: I won't let you purchase a gun. And I'll lock up the kitchen knives if necessary. Both are easy fixes.

NAOMI: The point is I have no say in whose eyes I get. And I don't like it!

PETER: That's right, but maybe we could put in a request for a *good* person's eyes.

NAOMI: You can't negotiate that kind of thing.

PETER: Look, I'm sure the doctor would understand that we'd have to draw the line with cold-blooded killers.

NAOMI: What if he's dismissive, and makes a case for self-defense?

PETER: Screw the guy! We move on to another doctor.

NAOMI: Seriously, I don't give a rat's ass—even if it was self-defense. I'm not walking around with a murderer's eyes in me.

PETER: Of course! Any kind of murder- *totally unacceptable*. Look, maybe they've got some rules in place on who can donate organs.

NAOMI: Do they?

PETER: Let's find out.

(He picks up his cell phone, presses a button, and talks into phone.)

PETER: Siri, could Charles Manson have donated his corneas if he wanted to?

(She smacks at his phone—not seeing it well.)

NAOMI: Stop it. You're teasing me. *(Beat.)*. . . I want Josephina's eyes!

PETER: Your friend, Josephina?

NAOMI: Yes, she was a saint.

PETER: But she passed away.

NAOMI: She was such a good person. She sacrificed for everyone. I miss her so much.

PETER: She *was* a good person.

NAOMI: She would've wanted me to have her eyes. I know it.

PETER: She's been gone a year now. It's too late.

NAOMI: They have eye banks where you can store them. Dammit, I should've asked her. I could've asked her. Why didn't I ask her?

PETER: Honey, that ship has sailed.

NAOMI: Yes, but I could've seen the world through her eyes. . . I could've kept a piece of her with me. I miss Josephina. I want her eyes.

PETER: I'm sorry, Babe. This is tough, I see that. But you're a courageous woman.

NAOMI: Nonsense. I'm a woman going blind, and my back's up against the wall.

PETER: Look, this is all going to work out.

NAOMI: Easy for you to say. But I'm the one with the crappy eyes. Since I was a child, did you know a fortune teller told my mother that my eyes were going to be a lot of trouble?

PETER: I didn't know that.

NAOMI: I was only five, and already my eyes were giving off bad vibes to the fortune tellers. (*She speaks now with a strange gypsy-like accent.*) *"Do you see the eyes on this little girl? These are the eyes of a blind person."* She was talking about my eyes, Peter.

PETER: I don't believe in gypsy fortune tellers, and your eyes are beautiful!

NAOMI: They're not!

(*He goes to her, and wraps his arms around her.*)

PETER: You know all my friends tell me you have the most gorgeous eyes. You've heard them say it.

NAOMI: Yeah, but they don't have to see through them.

PETER: Your eyes are big and innocent.

NAOMI: Shut up.

PETER: And loving. So much love in those eyes.

NAOMI: They're *horrible* eyes.

PETER: That's not true.

NAOMI: Yes, it is! *(She breaks away from him.)* They're good for nothing.

PETER: Don't say that, Naomi. Please, *never* say that.

NAOMI: Why not?

PETER: Cause *those eyes* are the same ones that saw me when I was this chubby guy who couldn't dress for shit.

NAOMI: *(Smiling.)* You wore a lot of Miami Vice shirts back then.

PETER: Yeah, but I was no Don Johnson. And *those eyes* saw me struggling, barely scraping by, working as a sub teacher with no real career in place.

NAOMI: But I saw that your students loved you.

PETER: And so did you. Because *those eyes* saw past my sadness and swagger, and figured out there was a diamond stuck somewhere deep inside the lump of coal that I was.

NAOMI: You were pretty sad back then.

PETER: I was...

(He crosses to her, and again, wraps his arms around her. Looks deeply into her eyes.)

PETER: But *these eyes* had the vision to see that we could be good together when nobody else gave us a chance. . .

(PETER begins kissing her eyes now. Softly. Gently.)

PETER: Where would I be without these eyes I'm kissing now?

NAOMI: I bet you say that to all the blind girls.

PETER: Nope, just to this one blind, wife of mine.

(They kiss each other, a good kiss for a moment, and then break the kiss.)

NAOMI: You think this surgery will go well?

PETER: Not a doubt in my mind.

NAOMI: Me too. I'm ready to go now. Love you.

PETER: Love you too.

FADE LIGHTS.
END PLAY.

CHAPTER 4 — REDEMPTION

CHAPTER 4: REDEMPTION

The Japanese have a word, *"Kintsugi,"* which is a method of repairing broken ceramic items with gold. The idea behind this is that the cracks in an object are part of its history and should be kept visible and shiny. One could say that with the addition of the gold filling in these cracks, the object becomes even more beautiful (and valuable) *because* of its flaws.

As a therapist and a human being, I whole-heartedly embrace this philosophy—feeling that we humans also become more beautiful and valuable when we've fallen and have done things that led to "cracks" in our emotional, spiritual, and physical lives, and which must be gold-filled afterwards. All kinds of stumbles can lead to cracks in our personhood, from poor health, to failed business ventures and finances, to failed dreams, failed relationships, and poor choices that cause others to be disappointed in us. It is easy to see that the world can break us in many ways. However, if we choose to pick ourselves up and allow others to see the flawed, vulnerable, and frightened side of us, then perhaps we may be able to fill in these cracks with "gold." This enables us to learn from our failures and disappointments.

Some would call this "life experience." In living this way, we gain the wisdom to go forward, making better choices that will lead to happier and healthier lives. We can all find hope in the concept of *Kintsugi*, taking to heart the idea that a "cracked" person is more beautiful and valuable than an un-cracked person, but only after they are willing to shine it up with the gold of life experience, and let other people see it.

GLORY DAYS
A short play — Dramedy

CAST OF CHARACTERS:
PAUL- Late twenties, former star baseball player who has put on significant weight since graduating college.
KATE- Late twenties. Married to Paul. Kind yet assertive.

SETTING: An Apartment in Queens, N.Y.
TIME: Present. Evening.

Originally produced as part of **New York State of Mind—Volume I** at Actor's Workout Studio in North Hollywood, CA. under the title of *Reunion*. Opened on April 5th 2013. Directed by Ali Kendall.

The cast was as follows:
PAUL: Darren Mangler
KATE: Katy Pollock Iva

A revised version of the play—under the title *Glory Days* was produced as part of **New York State of Mind—Volume II** at Actor's Workout Studio in North Hollywood, CA. Opened on June 6[th,] 2014.
Directed by Conrad Dunn.

The cast was as follows:
PAUL: Ronnie Rose
KATE: Julie Dolan

GLORY DAYS

An overweight young man– PAUL - swings a baseball bat in his small living room. There's a high-school yearbook that lies open on the coffee table in front of the couch. PAUL takes one last swing with the bat, and suddenly grabs for his shoulder as if he's in a great deal of pain.

PAUL: Aaagh! Dammit!

(An attractive woman in her late twenties- KATE- enters the room quickly. Observes PAUL rubbing his shoulder.)

KATE: Are you okay?

PAUL: Damn shoulder.

KATE: Are you taking your Glucosamine?

PAUL: Yes, I'm *taking my Glucosamine.*

KATE: You picked a funny time to swing a bat. Shouldn't we be getting dressed? We want to look good for your reunion.

PAUL: Oh yeah. Forgot to tell you. I'm not going.

KATE: You want to cancel *now*? An hour before we're supposed to leave?

PAUL: No big deal. Plenty of people skip their stupid reunions. It's all a marketing thing anyway. *Reunions of America* picks my pocket for a few hundred bucks while I go and make polite bullshit conversation with knuckleheads I haven't seen in a decade, half of whom won't recognize me when I see them anyway.

KATE: Paul, what's gotten into you?

PAUL: You ever think that maybe there's a reason I haven't spoken to most of these people since I graduated? Why start now?

KATE: You said you wanted to see your old friends. You were excited to see your old friends. What happened here?

PAUL: Key word in that sentence: *"old."*

KATE: What are you saying?

PAUL: I'm older. They're older. We've outgrown each other.

KATE: You didn't say that last year when we went to my reunion. Remember? It was like I was in some kind of time warp with all those people from my past coming up to us. And for a moment I went back in time. We all did. It was like we were all back in high-school again and nothing had changed. You noticed it too. You commented on that.

PAUL: Baby, look at me.

(He lays both his hands on his extended belly.)

PAUL: *Everything's* changed.

KATE: Really? To me, you look like the same big teddy bear I married a few years back.

PAUL: Key word in that sentence: *"big."*

(Now, he pinches the excess weight around his belly. She comes towards him and gives him a warm hug.)

KATE: Sweety, you put on some weight. Is that what's going to keep you from going to this thing?

(He picks up his high-school yearbook from the table, and shows her, a picture of himself in uniform.)

PAUL: You remember this picture of me?

KATE: How sexy you looked in that baseball uniform. There's the proof that I married a stud.

PAUL: Sure. You're using the right tense. *"Looked"* with an e-d ending which indicates past tense.

KATE: Spoken like an English teacher with a heavy emphasis on the dramatic.

PAUL: You want some drama? How about the fact that your husband's a *sell-out. (Off her confused look.)* That's right. I'm a sell-out.

KATE: What are you talking about?

PAUL: Who would've thought that this guy in the yearbook . . . No, that *winner* in the yearbook, would go on to become some loser who teaches English to middle school kids in the Bronx.

KATE: And that makes you a *loser?* I don't think so. And did you forget that you coach those kids, and they hang on every word you say. They idolize you.

PAUL: Sure, but they're all twelve years old. And they'll grow up one day and realize what a loser I really was.

KATE: Stop saying that, you're a great coach!

PAUL: Sure. Those who can't play the game, they coach.

KATE: That's not so. You still play baseball.

PAUL: Honey, I chug beer in a slow-pitch, co-ed softball league. And even there, they stuck me on first base cause they know I can't run after a ball. Dammit, how lame is that?!

KATE: You have bad knees. We can't change that.

PAUL: And a bad shoulder, and bad wrists, and what the hell happened to that guy in the yearbook who was scouted by all the top baseball colleges in his senior year?

KATE: And *that guy*—played a year at ASU where I *scouted* him, and I decided that I wanted him to play on my team on a year round basis—for the rest of our lives. *(She smiles warmly at him, but he's not having it.)*

PAUL: Well there you go. A big congratulations to *me*-who managed to close the deal with *you- my wife.*

KATE: You don't sound too happy about that.

PAUL: How could I be-- when I was supposed to graduate, and turn pro? Now, how do I go back to my high-school buddies who knew a different me? A guy they respected,and who all knew I was going to turn pro. Instead, I show up and tell them I'm teaching little kids we say cat in thiscountry and not *gatto*.

KATE: Okay then, Paul. So what do you want to tell them about the last ten years of your life?

PAUL: Nothing, cause I'm not going.

KATE: You are going. *We* are going. And you'll see when you get there that this whole thing—

PAUL: —*I'm not going, Kate!* I'm an overweight, under paid teacher who's got friggin' joint pain so bad that it makes me feel like a goddamn eighty-year old man.

KATE: Yes, and you're taking vitamins and supplements for the inflammation.

PAUL: Screw that! I'm tired of taking that crap.

KATE: Fine, then maybe it's time we look into acupuncture, or I'll give you more massages. You love my massages.

PAUL: Yes, I do. And I appreciate that, honey, but this isn't what I'd imagined for myself.

KATE: You're making adjustments.

PAUL: To being fat and old.

KATE: *To life!* And you're not old. And we could all stand to lose a little weight around here. You're adjusting to life *now,* as it is. And that doesn't make you a loser. Would I choose to be with a loser? I think not.

PAUL: Stop that! Don't make this about YOU, Kate. This is about me.

KATE: No, it's not. *(She points to his yearbook photo.)*It's about this kid in the yearbook. The kid with the big dreams of being a baseball star.

PAUL: Let me tell you something. *That* kid had the world by the balls. That kid had a future.

KATE: That kid grew up, got married, and made some hard choices for himself.

PAUL: Yeah, and where the hell have they got me?

KATE: (*Beat. Thinking*) … Are you not happy with me? With the life we've made together?

PAUL: I am. I'm happy with you, Baby. You're the best, and I couldn't have made a better choice in a wife. But I'm miserable with myself. You get that?

KATE: I see that.

PAUL: And do you see that it's hard for me now to go back to these people who all expected me to become somebody. . . Somebody I'm not.

KATE: Key word in that sentence—*Expected*—a word similar to *believed*, a*ssumed*, or h*oped for*, but your knees, your joints, God, the universe; they all conspired to take you to a different place.

PAUL: Yeah, and it's not a happy place.

(He hangs his head down, as she picks up his yearbook and holds it in her hand, looking again at that picture in the book.)

KATE: Look, I don't want to go to the reunion with this kid in the book. I want to go with *you*. Honey, you love baseball, and I'm sorry that things didn't work out as planned. But you've made some really good choices too. You chose to teach and you're good at it. And you chose to coach and you love those kids. I've seen you with them. Seen the way you talk to them and the way your eyes light up around them when you tell them the things you learned about the game. The kind of things that only someone who's *played* the game could tell them. And, you make a difference in their lives, and my life. And you chose to love someone who loves you back with all her heart. And I know that it's not a professional baseball contract, Paul, but what you've got . . . it's not too shabby either. You might want to have a word with this kiddo in the book. I think he's a little stuck in the past. *(Hands him his yearbook.)* I'm going into the bedroom, and get dressed.

(She exits into the bedroom. He sits down on the couch, stares at his photo for a nice long moment, and then begins talking slowly to the picture of himself in the book.)

168

PAUL: Hey buddy. Number nineteen. I got more than a hundred kids a day that are depending on me to learn a language they're not very good at. And I coach some of those kids and teach them how to run bases, and hit and throw a ball like I used to do. So maybe one of them could go pro or wear Yankee pinstripes one day...

(KATE comes to the door of their bedroom. And though PAUL doesn't notice her standing there, she observes and listens to him.)

PAUL: ... I don't know why it happened that it couldn't be me, but it doesn't matter anymore. I've gotta work with what I got. And keep moving. And let me tell you something else. I get sex now, just about anytime I want— without a curfew, and with a woman who loves me no matter that I'm fat, or in pain, or stupid about things in my life that have been going pretty good. And you should really think about that, Kid. Think hard about that.

KATE: Why don't you come into the bedroom, Honey? And let's take a shower, and both of us get dressed. I have the feeling it's going to be a great night tonight.

PAUL: . . . Yeah, I think so. I really think so.

(He gently closes the yearbook, and follows her into their bedroom—as we. . .)

FADE LIGHTS.
END PLAY.

GRAVE KNOWLEDGE
A short play — Drama

CAST of CHARACTERS:

CHARLIE: mid 20's -30's. A United States marine-recently returned home from Afghanistan

ROBERTA: A young woman in her mid to late 20's. Catholic school teacher.

SETTING: A small graveyard in Queens, New York.

TIME: The year is 2010. Late afternoon.

Originally produced as part of *New York State of Mind— Volume I* at Actor's Workout Studio in North Hollywood, CA. Opened on April 5th 2013. Directed by Rickie Peete.

Cast was as follows:

CHARLIE: Chris Karmiol

ROBERTA: Susan Smythe Robertson

A revised version of the play was produced as part of *New York State of Mind—Volume II* at Actor's Workout Studio in North Hollywood, CA. Opened on June 6th, 2014. Directed by James R.W. Hiatt.

Cast was as follows:

CHARLIE: Chris Karmiol

ROBERTA: Catherine Mersereau

ALSO Produced at American Theatre of Actors in New York City. Opened on January 22nd, 2015. Directed by Freddy Gonzalez.

Cast was as follows:

CHARLIE: Eric Chaefsky

ROBERTA: Mariel Suriel

GRAVE KNOWELDGE

In a small graveyard, two gravestones stand close by one another. There are a half dozen or more empty beer cans that litter the ground below these stones. A young marine named CHARLIE—dressed in the standard camouflage sand-colored pants, shirt, and boots. He sits on a beach chair to the side of the gravestones. He appears to be listening to music thru his stereo headphones as he sips from a can of beer. Now, he pulls the headphones from his ears, and reaches down inside his backpack and pulls out a six-shot revolver. He holds the handgun up in the air and points it in the general direction of the audience, but tilted high above their heads.

CHARLIE: Hittum dead . . . in the head . . . with the lead. Bulls-eye, Sir! Squeeze!

(He lowers the gun, puts his beer down, and reaches back inside his bag for a ribbon with a Purple Heart medal attached. He examines it closely and walks over to his brother's gravestone.)

CHARLIE: Don't want your damn medal if you're not here to wear it for me.

(He slaps the medal down on top of his brother's stone, kneels in front of the marker, and begins talking to the stone—as if to his brother—with the gun still in his hand.)

CHARLIE: I miss you, Bro. Been thinking a lot about you and me and the plans we had. I signed up cause I needed a paycheck, not a medal. I wasn't looking to be a hero. You didn't get that?

(Beat. Takes a moment, as if he's listening for a response that doesn't come to him.)

CHARLIE: We went over there together like we did everything together, but we had an agreement, man. We were coming back together, but not like this. You screwed up, brother. You screwed up royally. That guy was dead out there! He didn't need your bullshit bravery. Why didn't you just leave him?! *(Beat. Again, it's as if he's listening for a response that doesn't come.)* Why can't you talk to me? I'd do anything to hear your voice again, but I can't. . .so I made a decision here. I want to be with you, Bro.

*(CHARLIE holds the gun up to his head and places the barrel of the gun behind his ear. He closes his eyes. He cocks the trigger so we hear **SFX: Click of the gun.**)*

ROBERTA *(OFFSTAGE)*: Yes, Sister. I'll have the room ready by tomorrow.

(CHARLIE opens his eyes, and stands up. He quickly stuffs the gun away into his back-pack. The young woman whose name is ROBERTA, enters carrying a dozen roses in one hand, and a cell phone in the other, and there's a back-pack loosely slung over her shoulder.)

ROBERTA: *(into cell-phone)* Yes, I'll have the walls decorated with their projects by tomorrow. That won't be a problem, Sister. Okay then, Blessings to you also.

(She ends the call, and puts the cell phone away in a pocket. She stares at CHARLIE as he's sipping from his can of beer again.)

ROBERTA: Hello.

(CHARLIE stares back at her silently and takes another sip of his beer. She observes all the empty beer cans scattered in front of the gravestones.)

ROBERTA: Are you okay?

CHARLIE: Don't I look okay?

ROBERTA: It's just that uh . . . it looks like . . . it looks like you're camping out or something.

CHARLIE: What's it to you?

(He observes her as she gathers up the beer cans and places them in a tidy pile between the two grave stones.)

ROBERTA: Nobody's come out to talk to you about the chair and stuff?

CHARLIE: Actually, it's been kinda quiet. Peaceful till you showed up.

ROBERTA: I'm sorry I interrupted you.

CHARLIE: I was starting to wonder if anyone remembers these people.

ROBERTA: Looks like a few of us do.

(She spots the Purple Heart lying on top of his brother's stone and reaches for it, and holds it up to him.)

ROBERTA: Was this yours?

CHARLIE: Nope. It was his.

ROBERTA: Is this a Purple Heart?

CHARLIE: What's it look like? Just leave it alone, would you.

(He takes the Purple Heart from her, and gently places it back on top of his brother's gravestone.)

ROBERTA: I've heard about them, but never seen one before. He was a brave person—

CHARLIE: —Yup, my brother was brave. He was an idiot too.

ROBERTA: May he rest in peace.

(She takes a single rose from her clutch of flowers and gently places it on top of his brother's stone. Then she places the rest of the roses in front of a stone that sits right beside CHARLIE's brother's stone.)

ROBERTA: I'm Roberta. I teach at the high-school across the—

CHARLIE: —St. Christopher's? You teach at St. Chris?

ROBERTA: You know my school. So you're from around here then?

CHARLIE: What's it to you?

ROBERTA: Well people tend to come from somewhere, and being as your brother's buried here, and you know my school—

CHARLIE: —Yup. We're from around here.

ROBERTA: Do you have a name? Usually when I introduce myself to somebody, I get a name back. That's how that usually works.

(He stares at her. She stares back at him.)

CHARLIE: . . . Charlie.

ROBERTA: That's a nice name. You have any family around here, Charlie?

CHARLIE: Hey look, if you're writing a book on me, than make it a mystery.

ROBERTA: Any friends you could call?

CHARLIE: A few. Could I use your cell?

(She takes her cell phone from her pocket— as if to offer it to him.)

CHARLIE: You got a long distance plan, right?

ROBERTA: Why?

CHARLIE: All my buddies are back in Afghanistan.

ROBERTA: Oh. Nobody local?

CHARLIE: Just him. *(Referring to his brother's grave.)* And he ain't had much to say lately.

(She puts her cell phone back into her pocket.)

ROBERTA: You know there's a V.A. Center not far from here, and they have programs set up to—

CHARLIE: —Not interested.

ROBERTA: You think your buddies would want to see you like this?

CHARLIE: Like what?

ROBERTA: Alone. Drinking in a graveyard.

CHARLIE: News flash, Roberta. Marines drink.

ROBERTA: I know a priest at my school you can talk to. He's really good with—

CHARLIE: —*Crazy people*? Forget it. And if you're thinking I'm crazy. Then you're the one who's crazy, 'cause I'm not.

ROBERTA: Nobody said you were crazy. I'm just a little worried is all. Sometimes people need help. Doesn't mean they're crazy. Far from it. Sometimes it's the really smart people that can look for help when they need it.

CHARLIE: So does that make me stupid if I don't want your goddamn help?

ROBERTA: I didn't say that. And you don't have to curse.

CHARLIE: And you don't have to be a pain in my ass, but here you are.

ROBERTA: So what's your plan then?

CHARLIE: I got a plan, but it don't involve you trying to fix me.

ROBERTA: I don't know about fixing anybody, but the news just ran a story that the V.A. hospitals are running these free groups for Vets like you coming home from the war zones, so you can talk about some of the things you've been through.

CHARLIE: Group therapy? Where we all sit around in a circle, telling our sad stories, holding hands, and patting each other on the ass for a job well done??

ROBERTA: What's your problem?! Why can't you be open to some help?

CHARLIE: Cause I ain't no charity case!

ROBERTA: It's *not* charity. More like payment for services you gave to this country. Why not think about it that way?

CHARLIE: You know what I think? I think you ought to mind your own damn business.

ROBERTA: *(Stung by his remark.)* Okay then. As you wish. I'll just get back to my business.

(She turns away from him and takes a piece of paper from her backpack, and then sets her backpack on the ground behind her. She goes to her gravestone and holds the paper against it. She whispers something inaudible to the stone. CHARLIE observes her whispering.)

CHARLIE: You praying for the guy?

ROBERTA: No, it wasn't a prayer.

CHARLIE: Catholics like to pray for the dead.

ROBERTA: I wasn't praying!

CHARLIE: Hey, don't get your panties in a bunch here. I ask one question about you, and what you're doing, and you get all freaked out, but you had no problem asking me- like a ton of questions.

ROBERTA: Okay then. You want to know about me. Then why not ask me something, instead of being a jerk.

CHARLIE: You ain't said a word about this guy you came to see.

ROBERTA: He was a priest. Taught P.E.

CHARLIE: And you had feelings for him?

ROBERTA: What was I thinking, right?

CHARLIE: I don't know. What were you thinking?

(She remains silent. Just staring at her stone.)

CHARLIE: Two people fall for each other, and it don't matter that he's a priest. Things happen.

ROBERTA: Yes, they happen all right.

CHARLIE: And where's your family?

ROBERTA: We're not close anymore. They kinda stopped talking to me when they found out I was—

CHARLIE: —dating a priest?

ROBERTA: *(Beat.)* That's it. Old fashioned Catholics.

CHARLIE: Religion screws up everything. Priests ain't supposed to date, but when they do, then they have to hide it, and then your parents go ballistic when they find out their little baby girl's all involved with this man of God, and then everything goes straight to hell.

ROBERTA: You're right, but what family you know that isn't screwed up? A lot of people I know aren't talking to their parents, their brothers, their sisters. Seems like these two guys *(She nods towards both gravestones.)* are the only family we have right now, and like you said—they're not much for conversations, huh? I don't know about you, but I get lonely sometimes.

CHARLIE: I'll drink to that, but then again, I'd drink to just about anything.

ROBERTA: I'll do you one better. I propose a toast.

CHARLIE: Huh?

ROBERTA: Let's make a toast to *family*.

(She takes a bottle of water from her bag, and lifts it up to make a toast. And he lifts up his beer.)

ROBERTA: To the people we miss so much. Always will they be remembered. Always will they be loved.

CHARLIE: *Always faithful.*

ROBERTA: What?

CHARLIE: *Semper Fidelis.*

ROBERTA: What's that?

CHARLIE: Marine expression. Forget it. Let's toast already.

(They tap their drinks together.)

ROBERTA: You think they know we're here? That we're talking about them?

CHARLIE: That's a stupid question.

ROBERTA: I think they're watching. Listening to us.

CHARLIE: Shut up.

ROBERTA: You're rude. I'm just trying to—

CHARLIE: —Stop trying already!

ROBERTA: It could be worse.

CHARLIE: Oh my God, you are so annoying.

ROBERTA: It could be you or me in those graves.

(She studies him for a reaction, but he gives none.)

ROBERTA: And then we never would've met. And that would've been a shame, Charlie.

CHARLIE: How's that?

ROBERTA: Cause you're a good person. Anyone can see that.

CHARLIE: You know what I see. I see that you're getting in way over your head here if you think—

ROBERTA: —You know what I think? I think you don't know anything about me.

CHARLIE: What's to know? You're a Catholic school teacher who grew up in the neighborhood. And now you teach at a school that's probably walking distance from the house you grew up in.

ROBERTA: Okay. Okay. You guessed right, but that still doesn't mean you know me.

CHARLIE: Sure, I do. You hang out all day with hormonal, punk-ass teenagers in heat. And I'm sure the pressure that the penguins put on you to keep these kids from getting into each other's pants can get awfully tough. How do you stand all that goddamn pressure, Roberta?

ROBERTA: You're mocking me.

CHARLIE: Damn straight! Seriously, what life have you—

ROBERTA: —I'm *pregnant!* With his child.

(She gestures towards her gravestone. She takes out the same paper she'd held out to the stone before, but now turns it over, revealing to Charlie—)

ROBERTA: —It's my sonogram. I wanted to show him what our baby looks like.

CHARLIE: Some priest.

ROBERTA: It was our first time. We only did it once. What were the chances I'd get pregnant? I was two months late with my period when I went to him, and told him I was scared. I'm regular as hell, but he said he didn't believe me, and that made me angry so I told him I wanted a real relationship, and not just a one night stand.

CHARLIE: But he was a priest.

ROBERTA: Right, but I thought he loved me, and there was a chance for us, but that was before he said he was *sorry* we'd had sex. That he'd been unfaithful to his vows. And then he asked me to forgive him for this sin we'd done.

CHARLIE: You see that—I told you religion screws up everything.

ROBERTA: I asked him if that's what it was to him—a *sin*? Just a mistake? And he didn't answer me, and it just made me more angry with him, with myself, with God. And then I did something I'm not proud of. I tried to force his hand and I threatened to tell others at the school what we'd done—idiot that I am. And the next day, we passed each other in the hall, and he hands me a note. *"Put in for transfer. Was accepted. Leaving tomorrow."* How cruel was that?

CHARLIE: This was not a stand-up guy.

ROBERTA: So he got in his car and drove off, but he didn't get far. Truck ran a stop sign. At least that's what they said happened. I'm not sure, Charlie, if that's the way it happened, or if he did something stupid, and turned his car into the truck . . . And if he did that . . . If he did that, then I'm responsible for his—

CHARLIE: —Stop it! Cut it out, would ya. Priests know.

ROBERTA: Know what?

CHARLIE: That if you kill yourself, than you're screwed. You blow your shot at heaven. And he's not gonna do that, cause he knows how this thing works.

ROBERTA: I don't know . . . maybe you're right. I don't know. I haven't been able to talk to anyone about it till now with you. I guess I've been too busy trying to figure out what I'm going to do when they find out I'm pregnant.

CHARLIE: *They*? You mean the nuns at St. Chris? This won't be good.

ROBERTA: They hid away the pedophile priests for years, but God forbid an unmarried teacher in a Catholic school gets pregnant. They'll fire me first, ask questions later. Where does that leave me? How will I pay my rent?

CHARLIE: Hypocritical bastards.

ROBERTA: I was stupid. A very stupid person, but I'd read about others giving up things and making sacrifices for love. There was even a king somewhere that stepped down from his throne so he could marry a common woman. He gave up his throne for the woman he loved. All my guy gave up . . . was *me*.

(She begins softly crying. And CHARLIE observes and moves closer, and awkwardly but tenderly puts a hand on her shoulder.)

CHARLIE: Look, I'm sorry it didn't work out.

ROBERTA: And I'm sorry for what happened to you.

CHARLIE: Here we are—two sad sacks sitting in a graveyard. How pathetic is that?

ROBERTA: Charlie, you came from Afghanistan and I came from across the street. And here we are together now.

CHARLIE: What are you saying?

ROBERTA: Maybe they saw us, and know we've hit a rough patch. Maybe they thought we should meet, and try to help each other—

CHARLIE: —Shut the hell up.

ROBERTA: This is all too weird to be an accident, don't you see? Look at the two graves- how close they are to each other.

CHARLIE: Just my luck I run into a person crazier then myself.

ROBERTA: I'm not crazy. This is real, and—

CHARLIE: —You're gonna tell me what's *real* with all your vast worldly experience?! Growing up in this town and making it all the way over to St. Chris? I mean look at you. You're a little Catholic school girl who got knocked up by a priest who didn't pull out fast enough, and you're shocked to find yourself pregnant, and that he left you. How old are you? What world did you grow up in? No don't tell me. I already know your world. It's the one where kings give up their thrones to marry you. Well—*real* life don't happen that way, Roberta. It happens like what happened to these two stiffs we came here to see. It's all random and senseless. With no goddamn purpose or meaning in it. Can't you see that?!

ROBERTA: I don't. And you're lying, Charlie. You've got to start telling the truth here.

CHARLIE: Stop pretending you know me, 'cause you don't know shit about me!

ROBERTA: But I want to know you, Charlie.

CHARLIE: Don't say that!

ROBERTA: Charlie, don't you want to be known?

(Her words linger in the air for a moment. CHARLIE turns his head away from her for a moment, as if remembering.)

CHARLIE: What I've seen over there. What I've done. Nobody should want to know me.

ROBERTA: If you could tell me, I wouldn't turn from you.

CHARLIE: *(Beat. Struggling.)* This Afghan boy, couldn't have been more than ten. He was coming towards me in an open field, and I yelled at him to stop where he was . . . I yelled at him: *"Open your coat, little man! Just open your goddamn coat and show me there ain't no bomb underneath your coat!"* But the kid just kept coming so I tried to shoot him in the leg, but I panicked and hit him high in the chest. He went down. No explosion. No nothing. I waited a minute, and then went out to him. There was no breath in him. No pulse. And nothing under his coat, but he had something in his hand. Two sticks he put together with a string. What was he doing with a cross? Everybody's Muslim over there. Why's he got a cross? A good luck charm? A gift for me? And I looked at that cross in his hand and thought *"Where's God in all this? Where's God in this shitty war?"* Where is He now?

ROBERTA: He's here . . . with us.

CHARLIE: I don't believe that. If there was a God—then we wouldn't be here like two idiots talking to stones planted in the ground.

ROBERTA: I don't understand it either. But I think maybe they're looking out for us now.

CHARLIE: God is *not* looking out for me. I killed a kid. And I wasn't there for my brother when he needed me.

ROBERTA: You think your brother would want to see you like this?

CHARLIE: Go back to your classroom, and sharpen your pencils.

(She stands before him. Defiant. She doesn't move.)

CHARLIE: You heard me. Get lost.

ROBERTA: Okay then. I'm done. I'll pick up my bag and go.

(She moves to get her backpack, but suddenly goes to CHARLIE's backpack instead, and reaches inside to retrieve his gun. CHARLIE sees this, and moves quickly to wrestle the gun away from her, until he's got the gun firmly in his own hand.)

CHARLIE: You knew I had this?

ROBERTA: Yes, and I heard everything you said before I got here. Now what are we going to do about it?

CHARLIE: *We're* gonna do nothing, but you're gonna get the fuck outta here.

ROBERTA: If your brother could see you now—what do you think he would say?

CHARLIE: I dunno. *"Who's this bossy bitch?"*

ROBERTA: That's a lie. He'd tell you to give me your gun.

CHARLIE: (*Laughing.*) So now you're telling me what my brother would say to me. You're unbelievable.

ROBERTA: You've got to let him rest. And he'd want you to rest too, but not like you were planning.

CHARLIE: I want you gone.

ROBERTA: And what if I stay? Are you going to shoot me too?

(He points the gun directly at her.)

CHARLIE: Is that what you want? (*Tableau.*)

ROBERTA: . . .Is that what *you* want? A murder-suicide here in the graveyard? Sure to be the lead on tonight's news, so I'm really tempted to stay. But okay, Charlie, you win. I'm going home. And you do what you want, but I'll be back in the morning. And when I come back here, if I find you dead- with a bullet stuck in your head, then I want you to know that I'll be calling all the papers and TV news people and telling them all about your sad, little story. Not for you—not for your sake, but so maybe somebody else can learn something from what you've been through, 'cause you obviously haven't learned anything from all of your vast *worldly experience.*

(She turns to exit, and begins walking away from him.)

CHARLIE: Wait—

(She stops, and turns back around to face him.)

CHARLIE: —What am I supposed to do?

ROBERTA: I don't know. What would your brother want for you now?

(Slowly, CHARLIE turns his eyes towards his brother's gravestone, and stares at it for a moment- as if he's listening. . . BEAT . . . And then a small smile breaks across his face, as if he's just heard something.)

CHARLIE: I hear him. I finally hear him.

ROBERTA: That's good.

CHARLIE: He's telling me: *"Don't be stupid. Don't let her leave . . . without you."*

ROBERTA: *(Softly.)* You want a minute?

189

(He nods "Yes" to her. And she puts out her hand to take his gun, and he hands it over to her. And then he kneels in front of his brother's grave, and begins speaking to the stone once again.)

CHARLIE: Hey Bro. I'm leaving this place for now, but I'm never leaving you . . . I'll remember you for what you did, and who you were. Always looking out for the next guy. And maybe now . . . for Roberta and me.

(CHARLIE slowly reaches for the Purple Heart he'd left on his brother's stone. He picks up his brother's medal, and holds it.)

CHARLIE: I'll take you with me. Everywhere I go, I'll take you with me . . . *Always faithful.* Loyal to the end.

(CHARLIE kisses the medal, and gently places it into his shirt pocket. ROBERTA picks up her backpack and his backpack as well. He stands, crosses to ROBERTA, and takes his backpack from her, and puts an arm around her shoulder, and she puts an arm around his waist. Together, they begin to exit- as we slowly. . .)

FADE LIGHTS.
END PLAY.

THE MISERY OF HOPE
A short play — Dramedy

NOTE: This play is in tribute to Frank Capra and his classic movie: "It's a Wonderful Life".

CAST OF CHARACTERS:
PHIL, mid-late 20's thru 30's, a severely depressed young man.
DA'MON, 40's. Well-built. Dressed in fashionable black suit with red tie. Articulate.
ANGELA, 40's. Stocky woman with pronounced N.Y. accent and attitude to match. She's dressed in comfortable (light-colored) sweat suit outfit

SETTING: Phil's Living Room.
TIME: The present. Midnight.

Originally produced as part of *New York State of Mind—Volume II* at Actor's Workout Studio in North Hollywood, CA. Opened on June 6th, 2014.
Directed by Kelly Patino.

Cast was as follows:
PHIL: Tony DeCarlo
DAMON: John-Paul Lavoisier
ANGELA: Patricia Canale

THE MISERY OF HOPE

A very depressed looking young man—PHIL—sits on his living room couch in his pajamas. He's got a phone in one hand and a bottle of anti-depressants in the other. He's in the midst of a conversation that isn't going very well . . .

PHIL: Please, Mary. Don't say we're not good together. We *are* good together and I feel like we're just getting started. Let's give it some more time . . . Yes, I know we've been together two years already. . . Okay, I'll take you out more. How about mini-golf? I know this great little course that has an awesome windmill . . . You hate my apartment? Well so do I, but you know I can't afford to move; you know that . . . Yes, I'll do therapy just like you asked me to. I'll join a depression group, and sit around with a bunch of other depressed guys, and learn from them! . . . No! I'm not being sarcastic! I really want to learn better ways to deal with my depression . . . Yes, you mentioned that I can start breathing deeper like you do in your yoga classes . . . And yes, I can take more long walks, and pay attention to the flowers. I'm telling you, I CAN BE HAPPY!!! . . . You want me to take my meds? I can do that! I've got the whole bottle of pills in my hand right now. And I'll swallow the whole damn bottle if you want me to. Is that what you want?! . . . Am I trying to emotionally blackmail you? NO! I was just saying I'll take my meds. I'll do anything you want—just give me another chance. Please, Mary, give me another chance.

*(**SFX: CLICK of a phone!** Phone goes dead. And PHIL slowly sets the phone back into the cradle, and sets down the pills.)*

PHIL: Dammit, what's wrong with me? This is a never-ending cycle of rejection. And now I'm alone, and I don't want to be alone. . . Dammit, I've screwed up everything I've ever tried to do in my life. . . *I wish I was never born. . .* cause I don't want to live a life like this. I don't want to be depressed. I don't want to be a—

DA'MON: (*Off-stage LEFT*) LOSER!!!

PHIL: (*Confused.*) *Loser?* That's what Mary called me. I'm even starting to hear things. (*Picking up the bottle of pills, he stares at it—as if trying to make a decision.*) I can't keep on going like this, feeling every day like I'm a BIG—FAT—FRIGGIN'—

ANGELA: (*Off-stage RIGHT*): —WINNER!!!

PHIL: Now, I'm hearing things in stereo. Some *winner* I am. I'm done with this! I've had enough pain.

(*He undoes the cap on the bottle of anti-depressants and pours a great handful of pills into his hand, and stares at them. Suddenly, a well-dressed, well built, sexy looking gentleman wearing a black suit and red tie—DA'MON— enters quietly from the LEFT side of the stage. DA'MON crosses and stands behind the left side of Phil's couch. He's not been seen until he suddenly taps PHIL on the shoulder.*)

PHIL: Aaaggh! Who the hell are you?

DA'MON: Funny—you should use the word *hell* in that sentence.

(Suddenly—A stocky woman named ANGELA—enters from the RIGHT side of stage, and crosses to right side of PHIL's couch, and she's also not seen by PHIL until she taps him on the shoulder.)

PHIL: Aaaggh! What in heaven's name is going on here?!

ANGELA: Funny—you should use the word *heaven* in that sentence.

(DA'MON and ANGELA now stand at opposite ends of the couch staring daggers at each other while PHIL stares at the both of them.)

DA'MON: *(Disgusted.)* Angela . . .

ANGELA: *(With equal disgust.)* Da'Mon . . .

PHIL: I don't understand. Who are you two?

DA'MON: He's a bright one.

ANGELA: Why don't you give him a break? This kid's obviously depressed. *(To PHIL.)* But don't worry, Sweety, I've come to help you.

DA'MON: Me too. *(ANGELA shoots DA'MON an odd look.)*

PHIL: Help me with what?

DA'MON: Do you recall the part about *"wishing you were never born."*

PHIL: Yes! And then you guys showed up. *(Thinking . . .)* Hold it a minute! I got it now! . . . This is just like the scene in that movie they play every year at Christmas—where Jimmy Stewart said those exact same words just before he jumped off the bridge.

ANGELA: My favorite movie EVER! It's why I volunteered for this job.

DA'MON: At least that guy had the courage to jump. So what have you got there inside your hand?

(PHIL opens up his clenched fist revealing a heaping handful of pills.)

DA'MON: Enough with the small talk. Let's get on with it.

ANGELA: Don't rush the kid. He needs more time to think about some of his other choices.

DA'MON: What other choices?! This is his last and *best* choice. Let's just help him finish what he started, Angela, and we'll both go home early tonight.

ANGELA: Slow it down, Da'Mon. He's vulnerable. He's thinking about a permanent solution to a temporary problem. *(To PHIL.)* You're just a young man, and you've got a lot of life to live, Sweetheart.

DA'MON: Oh please. Stop with the Pepsi commercial. And if you want to talk about a young man who's got a lot of life to live, then let's talk about his kid brother who had a million bucks in his pocket by the time he turned twenty-one. Now that's a kid with a whole lot of life to live.

PHIL: He's right. My brother blew out the twenty-one candles on his cake, and promptly blew off our relationship from that day forward. (*To Da'mon*) Hey, how do you know about my brother?

DA'MON: Is this guy for real?

ANGELA: We both know about you Phil. Your mother —God rest her soul was a Saint. Your father—to put it mildly—was a real *dick*.

DA'MON: Language, Angela.

ANGELA: Eat me, Da'Mon. (*To PHIL.*) Your father was an angry man who took out all of his anger on you and your family. It's part of the reason you see yourself as a loser.

DA'MON: Well thank you, Dr. Phil.

PHIL: No! That was good. I hadn't thought about it like that.

DA'MON: Well thank goodness, for the rush of insight you've had in the closing moments of your life. What's next? A deathbed confession!? Let's move on, already!

PHIL: Man, you're really in a rush. Geez, I've never had even one person take an interest in me, and now I have two. Can't we just take our time with this?

ANGELA: Sure, we can, little buddy. Time is all we have. So why don't you put the pills back in the bottle while we talk to you a bit here—like you said there's no rush.

(PHIL takes the encouragement and puts the pills in his hand back into the bottle.)

ANGELA: Have you got any hot Cheetos?

PHIL: No, but I've got some Pistachio nuts in the bowl over there.

ANGELA: Pistachios? Skip it. How about a beer? Coors light is preferable, as I'm watching my weight.

DA'MON: Watching your weight?! Do you know how many calories are in a beer?

ANGELA: Da'mon, nobody's asking you to count my calories. *(Back to PHIL.)* So you got that beer, Philly boy?

(PHIL nods his head and gets up to get her the beer during this next bit of dialogue.)

PHIL: He's got a point, Angela. I mean, from the looks of things, we both could stand to eat a bit healthier. Meanwhile, Da'Mon looks kinda buff.

(PHIL hands off the beer to ANGELA.)

DA'MON: *Kinda* buff? *(DA'MON flexes both his massive arms.)* I flex these two arms of mine, and it's like I'm giving somebody a twenty one gun salute.

PHIL: And you really know how to dress.

DA'MON: *(Adjusting his red tie.)* The tie's from Trump's collection.

PHIL: And your voice is deep and rich. It's almost like I'm listening to James Earl Jones in Star Wars.

DA'MON: *(Begins singing in a deep, rich voice.) "ON THE WINGS OF LOVE . . ."*

ANGELA: *(Attempts to speak in a very deep voice.) "Luke, I am your father!"* That was a great movie! You see how we're bonding over here?

PHIL: Sure, but I also see that Da'mon looks good, sounds good, and I'm thinking he probably knows his way around the ladies.

DA'MON: *Around* the ladies? I go right at them, Phil, and there's hardly a one that can resist my subtle charms.

ANGELA: *Subtle?* Yeah, like a freight train.

PHIL: No offense, Angela, but I sure could use a friend that knows his way around the ladies.

ANGELA: Hey, I know my way around the ladies.

(Both PHIL and DA'MON look at ANGELA—with a shocked expression.)

ANGELA: Cause I *AM a lady*, in case you hadn't noticed here, and so I know how women think.

PHIL: But Da'Mon seems like a guy I can trust. Hang out with.

DA'MON: Of course, you can. For a *little* while.

PHIL: Don't take it personal, Angela. I'm probably just looking for a father-figure.

DA'MON: —Come to Papa.

(DA'MON opens his arms wide and beckons PHIL to come to him—and when PHIL crosses to DA'MON, then he gets a strong bear hug from DA'MON.)

ANGELA: Let me give it to you straight here, Phil . . . A snake oil salesman will always dress well. They always want to look good, and sound good so they can sell you their cheesy product. Take my word on this. You don't want anything this cheeseball's selling.

DA'MON: Would I steer you wrong, Buddy?

ANGELA: Now, if you take a look at me, Phil. I'm the real deal.

(ANGELA guzzles the beer, and then crushes the can with her bare hand.)

ANGELA: And I've come here tonight to tell you that things will get better if you just hang in there.

DA'MON: Quit blowing smoke up this guy's butt. Let him be done with his crappy life already.

PHIL: He's right, Angela. I've got nothing to live for.

ANGELA: That's false! You have a job!

PHIL: That I hate!

ANGELA: In this down-turned economy, one's fortunate to have any—

DA'MON: —The man sells time shares in Guatemala.

ANGELA: Wooh. That is a shitty job.

DA'MON: Don't you have some kind of language code you have to abide by?

ANGELA: *De-code* this, Da'Mon.

(She shoots DA'MON the "double-gun salute;" flipping him the bird with both fingers on both hands.)

PHIL: Da'mon's right. Things really suck right now. I'm lonely, I'm depressed, and I'm barely surviving on my paycheck.

ANGELA: But you've got a job! Remember that, Philly boy! You've got a—

*(DA'MON snaps his fingers. **SFX: PHONE RINGS LOUDLY.** PHIL stares at the phone for a moment.)*

PHIL: It's after midnight . . . (*Picking up phone.*) Hello?. . . I'm fired?

(DA'MON smiles at ANGELA.)

DA'MON: *Had* a job, Angela.

(PHIL hangs up the phone.)

ANGELA: That was low, man. You just kicked this kid in his ass when he was already holding on to his nut sack.

PHIL: Now I'm jobless, depressed, and lonely. Oh my God, this is bad.

DA'MON: Not true. This is *horrible*. And this is the time when most people in your position just clock out. And I'm here for you, Phillip.

PHIL: *You're here for me?*

DA'MON: To help you punch out your card.

ANGELA: Phil, it's time you start looking for the silver lining in the cloud formations here.

PHIL: What silver lining? What are you talking about?

ANGELA: First of all—you hated that job. It was beneath you.

DA'MON: —Oh please. Don't sell the kid Hamburger Helper and call it Filet Mignon. He has every right to die with some dignity.

ANGELA: How about trying to *live* with some dignity? And I have some great ideas about how to do that which I'd like to share with my new friend.

DA'MON: *(Bored. Yawning.)* S.O.S.

PHIL: *S.O.S.?*

DA'MON: SAME-OLD-SOUP. She just reheats it. (*To ANGELA.*) Don't you ever change it up?

ANGELA: If it ain't broke, then I don't have to fix it.

DA'MON: Oh, please! This is where she goes into her tired old propaganda pitch about how you should just *look on the bright-side* of this debacle that has become your life. And then she'll try and convince you that *the glass is really half full*, if you only just hold it up to the right light. And worst of all, she's going to finish it up with (*Begins laughing.*) Get this now (*Laughing harder.*) . . .There's a *blessing in disguise* if you just look for it. C'mon Phillip, you've heard these corny, hackneyed clichés all your life. And you've lived enough life to know that they mean nothing to a smart guy like yourself.

ANGELA: Ignore him, Phil. Every day is a new day- another chance to *live, laugh, and love.*

DA'MON: *Another* cliché.

ANGELA: You live in HOPE, you die in despair.

DA'MON: And *another.* You look up the word "corny" in a dictionary, and you'll find a picture of Angela's face right next to it.

ANGELA: Yeah, and if you look up the word— (*ANGELA's struggles to find an accurate word to describe DA'MON until-*) —pretty boy, chiseled chin, Adonis—

DA'MON: —Aha! So your true feelings about me come out.

ANGELA: Enough! (*Back to PHIL.*) Enough with words. I've prepared a *song* that I'd like to sing for you now, Philly boy.

DA'MON: No! You will NOT sing *"The Sun Will Come Out Tomorrow."*

ANGELA: Oh yes, I will. It's a beautiful song. Filled with hope.

PHIL: Then don't sing it! I don't have any more hope for a brighter tomorrow.

ANGELA: But why Phil?

PHIL: You're seriously going to ask me that question?

DA'MON: And I'd like to answer that one for you, Phil. (*Places a comforting hand on PHIL's shoulder, but turns to ANGELA.*) Angela, you just don't get it, do you? This man had *dreams*. Dreams of what he was to accomplish with his time here on earth. But the world has conspired against him to take this man's dreams, and smash him over the head with them. His dreams now sit in a pet-store window like some *homeless puppy* barking at him—day after day—year after year—taunting him about what might've been.

ANGELA: Barking like a homeless puppy in a window? An interesting visual there, Da'Mon.

DA'MON: That's right. All his dreams have come to nothing but a pile of ashes. And to his credit, he's come to understand that it's better to choose to die a quick and relatively painless death rather than keep on living a slow and painful life.

ANGELA: You must not listen to him. You must *keep hope alive.*

DA'MON: A bit desperate, don't you think?

ANGELA: (*Chanting loudly.*) *Keep hope alive! Keep hope alive! Keep hope alive!*

PHIL: Angela, stop chanting. I've been doing that my whole life, and where's it got me?

DA'MON: I'll take that question too, Phil. *NO-where!!!* You've been forever hoping but never realizing your dreams. And who wants to live that kind of miserable life?

PHIL: You're right, Da'mon. It's like I've been living my entire life with the misery of hope.

DA'MON: Bravo! *The misery of hope.* I like the ring of that. You won't mind if I use that phrase to encourage other lost souls like yourself- would you?

PHIL: Why not. It's the truth.

DA'MON: (*to ANGELA*) You see that Angela. This is Phil's truth. And the truth must be spoken. Now you see why he doesn't want to hear your lousy song?

ANGELA: I see nothing of the sort.

DA'MON: Admit it, you do see it! And you know that his future's already passed him by, and all he's got left now is this lousy, rotten present moment so that he can finish what he started. And Phil, there's not a man on this planet that would blame you for making this choice.

ANGELA: Maybe there's not a *man* on this planet—

DA'MON: I just said that. Angela. Let's move on already. Phil, go ahead and take the pills. They go down quicker with a shot of whiskey if you've got a bottle.

(DA'MON offers PHIL the bottle of pills. And PHIL pauses to consider this option once again.)

PHIL: I don't drink whiskey.

DA'MON: No shocker there. Okay, enough talk already.

(DA'MON picks up the bottle of pills and firmly presses it into PHIL's hand. PHIL looks at the pills and is about to pour them out into his free hand when. . .)

ANGELA: Hold it, Phil! Maybe there's not a man who would blame you, but what about that homeless puppy that Da'Mon spoke of?

DA'MON: What are you talking about?

ANGELA: You know the one that was sitting in the window of a pet store? Looking for someone to love him . . . What about that little creature?

DA'MON: Stick to the point, Angela, and stop going off on tangents.

ANGELA: Oh, I'm right on point here, Da'mon.

(ANGELA imitates a dog and puts her hands up by her face-as if they were paws, and begins barking at PHIL.)

ANGELA: RUFF! RUFF! . . . RUFF! RUFF! RUFF!

DA'MON: What are you doing?

ANGELA: Hey little buddy, do you remember a homeless puppy that was sitting in a pet store window? And he was barking at you?

PHIL: . . . Are you talking about Rocky?

ANGELA: Yes. And that pet store was going out of business the next day, and nobody had claimed him. Poor little guy . . .

PHIL: He was left behind—sitting in that crappy cage, barking at me, staring at me with those big brown, bulging eyes.

(ANGELA pulls out a photograph from her pants pocket and looks at it. She hands the photo over to PHIL.)

ANGELA: Are those the *bulging eyes* of which you speak?

PHIL: That's him! This was my favorite picture of Rocky. Looking at me with his tongue sticking out like that.

(*DA'MON leans in to catch a glance of the photo as well.*)

ANGELA: Yes! His tongue was too big for his mouth, and it always stuck out to the side. Kind of like this, Phil?

(*ANGELA demonstrates, and sticks her own tongue out of the left side of her mouth. PHIL smiles now.*)

PHIL: Yes! I loved that tongue. And his cork-screw tail, and that little under-bite he had.

ANGELA: Yes, that under-bite. Did it look like this?

(*Again, ANGELA demonstrates an under-bite with her lower jaw pushed forward showing only her bottom teeth.*)

PHIL: That's exactly how Rocky looked!

(*In frustration, DA'MON snatches the picture out of PHIL's hand and stares at it.*)

DA'MON: A PUG! You brought him a picture of his own damn pug?!

PHIL: Hey! You watch how you talk about Rocky. He was like a son to me. Always giving me kisses.

ANGELA: That's right, Phil. So many little kisses he gave you. And then there were the big sloppy ones—especially in the mornings to wake you up.

DA'MON: For Pete's sake, you probably had some food stuck to your face from the night before —

PHIL: No! Those kisses were for real, cause he loved me, and they were the BEST kisses I ever had in my life.

DA'MON: From your sloppy, smelly, dog?! How *pathetic*, is that?!

ANGELA: You just don't get it, Da'Mon, do you? Rocky gave this boy unconditional love. And it didn't matter if he was broke, or working a crappy job, or living life like a couch potato.

PHIL: You're right. He just loved me for who I was. And all he wanted back from me was to hold him, feed him, and give him belly scratches . . .

DA'MON: *Belly scratches?!* This is ridiculous! Let's get back to your miserable life, and your hopeless future. And skip this sentimental bull-crap with your ugly mutt.

PHIL: What?! What'd you call Rocky?

DA'MON: Give me a break, I mean look at this picture. Anybody would tell you that this face. This face . . . with the tongue, the eyes, the under-bite is soo ugly—

ANGELA: —Finish his sentence, Phil. *Rocky was soo ugly that—*

PHIL: —he was *beautiful*. And he was my angel . . .

ANGELA: Yes, he was. And Rocky's spirit is still with us today, cause the memory of him has not died. And it never will.

DA'MON: How low can you go, Angela? To toy with his emotions like this? You should be ashamed of yourself.

ANGELA: There's no shame in telling the truth. And the truth must be told here. Phil's truth. *(Turning back to PHIL.)* And what would Rocky say about this thing you wish to do, tonight, Phil?

PHIL: He'd want me to . . . live.

ANGELA: Yes, he would. And Phil, I have something else for you.

(ANGELA pulls a crinkled up, grease-stained brochure from out of her pocket, and hands it over to PHIL.)

ANGELA: It's a little greasy from the BBQ spare ribs the other night, but I think Rocky would've wanted you to have this.

PHIL: *(Reading from brochure.)* An adoption agency for dogs?

ANGELA: And they're looking for volunteers. They need people to rescue dogs that have been rejected, and are down and out, and have nobody to care for them, dogs that are—

PHIL: —Like *me*?

(ANGELA nods her agreement.)

DA'MON: Unbelievable! Whatever happened to the misery of hope, or punching your clock, or swallowing the damn bottle of pills?

PHIL: Now why would I want to do that—Da'Mon, when I just found a reason to live? You obviously don't get me, so why don't you just go to HELL?

(*DA'MON is shocked. He can't believe he's been sent back to hell.*)

ANGELA: Aw—so sorry, Da'mon. I mean it was a great presentation and all. And you look so good. And that's a really great tie, was it from the "You've Been Trumped" collection, I believe, isn't it? But it's time to step away, don't you think?

DA'MON: Screw you both!

ANGELA & PHIL: *STEP AWAY, DA'MON!!!*

(*DA'MON huffs and puffs as he exits. ANGELA and PHIL crack up into hysterical laughter. Until ANGELA crosses to PHIL and puts an arm around him.*)

ANGELA: So what have we got to eat, little Buddy?

PHIL: There's some left-over pizza in the fridge. It's two days old, but it should still be good.

ANGELA: Only two days? Sounds great! And Phil, I happen to have a DVD of that Frank Capra classic.

(*She pulls out a DVD from her pocket, and hands it to PHIL.*)

PHIL: (*Reading from DVD box.*) "*It's a Wonderful Life*" Angela, this is great! We can watch it together while we eat the pizza.

ANGELA: We sure can. And just so you know, Philly boy, all of my really close friends . . . they call me *Angel*.

(*They share a knowing smile between them- as we slowly begin to. . .*)

FADE LIGHTS.
END PLAY.

SAYING GOODBYE
A short play — DRAMA

CAST OF CHARACTERS:
FATHER: Older man. Proud. Fragile. Weakened but still has some fight left in him. Estranged from his son.
SON: Mid-late 20's. Proud, headstrong. Finally got his life on track. Deeply conflicted feelings for his father.

SETTING: Father's living-room
TIME: The present.

Originally produced as part of **Today's the Day—A Night of 1-Acts** at Actor's Workout Studio in North Hollywood, California.
Directed by Conrad Dunn.

The Cast was follows:
FATHER: Paul Surace
SON: Holger Moncada, Jr.

SAYING GOODBYE

Fragile FATHER sits in his comfortable living room chair with a well-worn blanket covering his legs. He adjusts his glasses, as he reads the newspaper. A moment passes, and then there's a knock on the door.

FATHER: *(Calling out.)* Door's open!

(SON walks through the door. FATHER lifts his eyes from the paper, and looks at his SON intently—silently staring.)

SON: Hey Pop, were you going to say something here or just keep looking at me? *(FATHER continues to stare.)* Shit. Nobody ever told you it's not polite to stare? . . . Back in high school, they'd say you were *mad-dogging* me right now, and that's how a lot of fights got started. That what you want tonight, Pops, a fight?

FATHER: *Nothing!* I hear *nothing* from you for how many years is it, and you want me to welcome you back with open arms?

(Beat of silence.)

SON: It's been awhile . . . yeah.

FATHER: Ya think?! *(Goes back to reading his paper.)*

SON: Okay. Okay. Look, what I have to say won't take long.

(FATHER sets the paper back down on his lap, and gives his SON his full attention.)

FATHER: You're here to make an apology—don't cut it short.

SON: That's not why I'm here.

FATHER: Then why are you here?

SON: I've got to report, tomorrow.

FATHER: *Report?* Whatta you talking about?

SON: They needed a few good men. I needed a job.

FATHER: The Marines? You join the Marines now with this goddamn world on the verge of blowing itself up? *Now,* you go and join the Marines?!

SON: Okay, you made your point.

FATHER: Where they sending you?

SON: I don't know. Middle East somewhere.

FATHER: Uh huh. There you go. So you're off to fight in a war that don't have no end.

SON: Look, I thought you might want to know.

FATHER: Know what? That my kid might be lizard food in a few weeks? You think I want to know that?

SON: Some parents might.

FATHER: *(Almost proudly.)* Well, I ain't that parent.

214

SON: No, you're not . . . Okay then, this was a bad idea. I gotta go.

(SON turns to leave.)

FATHER: Where you going?

SON: Somewhere you're not.

FATHER: Sit your ass down.

SON: I don't take orders from you.

FATHER: I said, *sit your ass down!*

SON: And I said, I don't take orders from you.

(Tableau. FATHER changes his tone, and speaks softly.)

FATHER: . . . I looked for you.

SON: And I hid from you, but I'm not hiding anymore.

FATHER: I hired some piss-poor detective—the idiot couldn't find Mickey Mouse in Disneyland.

SON: Must've been some cheap-ass detective.

FATHER: Where'd you go?

SON: Doesn't matter. I'm here now.

FATHER: Did you *find* Jesus?

SON: Didn't know He was lost. Why'd you ask me that?

FATHER: Cause all these morons find *religion,* when life kicks them in the ass, and then they come crawling back home.

SON: First off, I'm not a *moron*, and my wife- she's not a religion, though she'd probably take that as a compliment.

FATHER: You're married now?

SON: That'd be a yes.

FATHER: Must be a saint if she can put up with the likes of you.

SON: You know what we called mom, right? *Mother Teresa.*

FATHER: You're mom *wasn't* no Saint.

SON: Pretty close. My wife's a good woman too. She told me to come back and talk with you.

FATHER: You need someone to tell you that?

SON: Yeah, I did.

FATHER: Why's she not here?

SON: She wanted to come, but I told her *"No. Let's see how things go".*

FATHER: So how's this going?

SON: Like what I expected.

FATHER: And what were you expecting?

SON: It's never been easy trying to talk to you.

FATHER: Look, I tried to help you. I tried teaching you my business.

SON: I *hated* your business. Let's not go there, Pop.

FATHER: I tried to toughen you up. To make a man out of you, but you walked off the job.

SON: Pop, please. I don't want to go there with you.

FATHER: I was grooming you to take over. And you have one bad night, and the next morning, you're gone. Poof! You run away from me.

SON: You remember that night?

FATHER: Sure. You were on the job.

SON: You had me out there watching your damn cement dry.

FATHER: That's right, so the kids don't come around and put their hands in it. Or they get the sticks and write their names—so you gotta be there.

SON: Sure, 'cause then you've got to re-pour the sidewalk, if I don't chase them away, but do you remember the neighborhood?

FATHER: Yeah. What about it?

SON: It's the same place where they shot a guy the week before. They took five bucks from the guy, and shot him dead.

FATHER: People get shot all the time. What's your point?

SON: You had me out there *alone*—with a fucking flashlight—after midnight. And you didn't call. You went to bed early that night. And that's when I knew.

FATHER: *Knew?* Knew what?

SON: That's when I knew.

FATHER: Whatta you talking about?

SON: You know what I'm talking about.

FATHER: I *know* you're a prickly kid. I told your mother that—*"He's too damn sensitive"*—I told her that all the time.

SON: So I was sensitive, and you didn't give a shit. So how are we gonna make that work?

FATHER: It has to work, because we're family. And a son don't leave his father.

SON: You left ME there that night

FATHER: I left you *on the job!*

SON: You don't get it do you?

FATHER: Get what?!

SON: You drove me away! Look, I gotta go. My wife's waiting.

FATHER: You hiding her from me?

SON: What?

FATHER: You ashamed of me?

SON: NO! No. She doesn't need to be in the middle of this.

FATHER: Then call her. I want to meet her, *today.*

SON: I said I'm not putting her in the middle of this. This is just between you and me, don't you think?! *(Apologetic now.)* Look, Pop, maybe next time when you're feeling better.

(FATHER waves him off and turns his face away from his SON.)

FATHER: There ain't gonna . . . There ain't gonna be a next time.

SON: Who told you that? Your doctors said that to you?

FATHER: They don't have to tell me nothing. I see it in their faces.

(FATHER turns back to SON. He gathers himself up as if to make a pronouncement...)

FATHER: I got no *regrets* with you.

SON: Why you telling me that, when I didn't ask?

FATHER: In case you were wondering.

SON: You're a real *piece of work,* you know that?

FATHER: That why you came back? For some kinda confession? Cause I ain't got nothing for you.

SON: Okay then. How about I make a confession.

FATHER: I look like your priest? *(Smiles slyly.)* Or you just looking for a blessing?

SON: . . . It wasn't my job to make you happy or prove myself to you. You want to be miserable, then so be it. Help yourself. I should've accepted that, and got on with my own life.

FATHER: That's it? That's your big confession?

SON: That's it.

FATHER: It's *selfish.* Where's your *family* in that?

SON: We might have a different definition of that word.

FATHER: Only one definition of that word, and you're looking at him.

SON: Pops, I don't accept that anymore.

FATHER: Look, I did my job with you.

SON: What job did you do? What do you even know about me?

FATHER: I know more about you then you know about yourself.

SON: You never even saw me. I was *invisible* to you!

FATHER: Bullshit! I seen parts of you that you never seen in the mirror.

SON: Well you should've held that mirror up to yourself once in awhile, and catch a glimpse of who you are, and what you put me through . . . SHIT! This is NOT why I came back. I don't want to dig up the past with you, cause we can't change it. I just want to let it go.

FATHER: So I'm gonna ask you one more time. Why did you come back to me?

SON: Cause when I go out there—these feelings I got inside me, I don't want to take them with me.

FATHER: . . .You hate your father? (*SON is silent.*) I'm asking you now, if you got hate in your heart for your father?

(*SON stays silent. FATHER understands now why his son came back to him, and it seems like he's suddenly got the wind knocked out of him. . .*)

FATHER: Well that's on you! Cause I done nothing but try and give you a life, that anyone else would be—

SON: —SHUT UP! SHUT UP, you stupid old man! Stop defending! I didn't come here to blame you, so stop blaming me for what I felt for you my whole life. Who's at fault for this? Who's to blame for the two of us now, who don't know a damn thing about each other? Who's at fault? You? Me? Mom's gone now. You want to put it on her?! Shit, it doesn't matter anymore. All that matters now is . . . All that matters . . . *is now*. And I just came back . . . to sit with you . . . and try to get to know you different than before.

(SON sits down and takes his FATHER's hand in his own. FATHER simply stares at his SON's hand that covers his own. Beat.)

SON: . . . So maybe then we could say good-bye.

FATHER: *(Emotional. Fragile.)* But you just came *home*, Son . . . You just came home.

SON: You're right. I am home. And I'm gonna sit for awhile.

(FATHER reaches out with his free hand and places it on top of his SON's hand.)

FATHER: I want things *different* between us.

SON: Me too.

FATHER: Cause I'm your father.

SON: I know that, Pop.

FATHER: And a father don't leave his son.

SON: I know that too, Pop.

FATHER: And I never left you.

SON: That's right. You never did. Thank you.

FATHER: No, don't thank me. I was just doing my job with you.

SON: Pop, I'm gonna thank you if I want to.

FATHER: Okay then. What are you thanking me for?

SON: For never leaving. . . For doing the best you could.

FATHER: *(Smiles.)* You got that, huh?

(SON smiles back at him, and nods as if to say "Yes.")

FATHER: That's good . . . I'm gonna rest my eyes for a minute.

SON: Sure, Pop. Get some rest.

(FATHER leans back in his chair and closes his eyes. SON pulls the blanket gently over his FATHER's legs, and then slowly but deliberately, rests his hand gently over his father's hand-- as we slowly--)

FADE LIGHTS.
END PLAY.

About the Author

Paul Richard Surace, LMFT

Paul Surace is a dramatist, producer, actor, teacher and Licensed Marriage and Family Therapist. He has earned two Master's Degrees (Communications & Clinical Psychology), and has even put in five years as a stand-up comic. As a Walt Disney Company Fellowship winner, he wrote and developed several screenplays with his writing partner, one of which (*Bullies*) went into development. A second screenplay (*Grave Knowledge*) also went into development with Hollywood producer, Lynda Obst.

Within the last five years, Surace has written over 30 short plays, some of which have been produced in New York City—including *Grave Knowledge* at the American Theatre of Actors. His play, *The Last Call*, was produced at the Stella Adler Theatre in Hollywood. During that same five-year period, he also wrote and produced three installments of his evening of original one-act plays called *New York State of Mind* to mostly sold-out audiences. Many of these plays appear in this book. Surace's full-length Christmas dramedy, *Merry Christmas, Miss Molly,* was produced on theatre row in New York City. Another full-length, family drama, *Homecoming,* was produced at the Sherry Theatre in North Hollywood.

As a teacher, Surace taught undergraduate students at *St. John's University* in New York and *Pepperdine University* in Malibu, California. He also spent a number of years teaching younger, middle-school, and high-school students in the Los Angeles Unified School District. As a therapist, Paul currently teaches classes in Communication, Anger Management, and Work Stress Reduction and for decades has been counseling young teens, adults, couples, and families. This is Paul's first published book of plays, but he promises that there will be several more to follow.

Author Paul Surace with Rocky (middle) and Rocky's friend who stopped by for a play date.

Author's Request

If you enjoyed *HEARING VOICES*, I'd be very grateful if you'd post a comment or short review onto Amazon's website. Your support really does make a difference in spreading the word and getting the book to others who might also enjoy it.

To *post a comment*, go to the website of *Amazon.com*, click on "Books" in the drop-down menu, then type in my name or the book's main title (HEARING VOICES) in the search window. When you see my book cover, *click* on it to get to my full book page and then scroll *way* down to a small orange box that says *"Write a customer review."* Click on that. It will ask for your Amazon Sign-In information (email and password). Once you're in, a box opens. Type in your comment.

Thank you! — Paul Richard Surace, LMFT

Contact Information for the Author:
paulnywriter@gmail.com
www.CandlelightPlays.com

www.ingramcontent.com/pod-product-compliance
Lightning Source LLC
Chambersburg PA
CBHW022015090426
42739CB00006BA/136